IT'S YOUR TURN NOW!

Principles of Preparation for Promotion

ALMA GORDON BAMBERG

IT'S YOUR TURN NOW!
Copyright © 2018 by BAMMIN

All rights reserved. No part of this publication may be reproduced, stored in a retrieval system or transmitted in any form or by any means – except for brief quotations in printed reviews, without prior permission from the author.

ISBN-13: 978-0-692-09463-1
ISBN-10: 0-692-09463-6

Dear Reader,

As I meditated on writing this book, I thought, what gives me the right to tell anyone *"It's Your Turn Now?"* I thought, what entitles me to share the words of this book with others, especially my sisters? As I pondered those questions, I was reminded of a passage of Scripture where the Apostle Paul was addressing those in Corinth who were questioning his apostleship. He told them, *"Even if others think I am not an apostle, I certainly am to you. You yourselves are proof that I am the Lord's apostle"* (1 Cor. 9:2 NLT). Paul understood the people whose lives he had impacted for the kingdom of God was all the proof he needed to authenticate his message.

Paul's response to his critics helped me realize, true validation can only come from people whose lives you've impacted. The many people who had previously expressed to me how my life and ministry had in some way impacted their lives, began to flood my mind. And I thought, they are my **PROOF**. They are the ones who can truly endorse the message of this book.

With that in mind, I've asked a few of my sisters to share their testimony of how I've helped them to take their turn in life. As you read their testimonies, you'll see how taking your turn covers a wide variety of opportunities to be promoted in life. I pray you are able to identify with at least one of their testimonies as proof that you're not alone and if I could help them take their turn, just maybe this book will encourage you to TAKE YOUR TURN, too!

"Igniting & Fanning Flames of Hope and Possibility",

Testimonials for
IT'S YOUR TURN NOW!

"The time was the year of 2000, a dry, starved season in some areas of the land, bountiful in others. It was at this time that a young woman of honorable reputation and standing, awoke to a normal day of routine. She rose early, prayed to the Father that great things would happen that day for her expectation was that she might be used mightily. On her way to work, her thoughts still on her prayer time, walking a path she had walked so many days before, she stumbled upon something that lay in the road before her. It did not seem so pretty nor did it seem dangerous, and something within her stirred as she looked upon this vessel. Inexplicably, she was drawn to it, bent down, and very carefully picked it up as she could see there was some *damage*. The vessel was dirty, chipped in some places but the young woman could see beyond all of that and saw something of beauty, you see she had an eye for things of value that others seemed to *discard*. There was something unusual about this vessel, it was one-of-a-kind and she knew that it belonged to some collection, but somehow had become *misplaced*. "I wonder what the history of this vessel is," she thought. "I will take it with me and refurbish it." She did just that. She took the vessel home, washed it, repaired it, polished it, and then began to fill it up by reason of use. "Yes, this is its original purpose, to be used by others that might enjoy its uniqueness." The vessel was one of many that this woman refurbished and freely shared with others, all of them unique and so *her eye for things of value* became the very answer to her prayer. She was used mightily ever after.

Alma Gordon Bamberg, you are the young woman in the story. I am that vessel that you found some 18 years ago at a Sunday morning service; *seemingly discarded and out of place, spiritually dirty, and emotionally broken*. I came to the altar for prayer with head down, teary-eyed, and you looked at me thoughtfully as though you were seeing pass me, a look full of meaning unknown to me. I know now that it was not your hands, but the hands of God made flesh through you that found me and nurtured my spirit back to life. I was nurtured back so well, that now, I teach and nurture other broken vessels. And that is what you are to me—a little bit of Jesus made flesh in the Earth. I am grateful for your discernment and obedient heart. Keep taking the dirty, dusty roads as there are so many more misplaced vessels needing to be found. It is their TIME and their TURN. I honor you as my Pastor, Mentor, Naomi, Sister, and Friend in Christ."

- *From a Sister DAMAGED, DISCARDED, and MISPLACED*

"Back in June 2001, I was invited to one of your *Sisters of Destiny* women's fellowship. When I saw your welcoming smile I immediately felt a connection. Little did you know how broken I was. I had NO self-worth. I was suffering from deep depression that literally made me want to end my life. I thought I could just go to sleep and never wake up. I was hurting silently! But there was something about you, Pastor BAM. You have a presence about you that's warm and ultimately was the reason I joined Spirit and Truth World Outreach Church shortly after our first encounter. I just felt like *you saw me*. I mean, you didn't look over me. You validated me. You counseled me. And *since that day forward I've been delivered from depression.* All the glory belongs to God! But Pastor BAM, you really do make a difference in my life and I thank you for that!"

- From a Sister Battling DEPRESSION

"Early 2013, my spiritual Mom, Sister Bam started a series called "Dream the Impossible Dream". OH MY GOSH, it was on FIRE! She spoke about the importance of calling those things that are not as though they were. I remembered her saying, "Just do it!" That resonated with me like never before. All I know is that I could hardly contain myself that Sunday in service. I had recently told God that it was time for me to do something different. I began feeling a sense of discontentment with where I was in life. I felt like I was supposed to be doing something different or more with my life; possible changing jobs, or working for someone else. I felt like God was telling me, "it's time to MOVE!". Oh yes! I was getting ready to move, but not like I thought. I later realized, I was being setup to work for myself! For years I knew I wanted to start my own business but I didn't know what I wanted to do. And if I didn't know what I wanted to do, I sure didn't know when. But when Pastor Bam spoke that Word that Sunday morning, my impossible dream felt possible.

Of course, fear showed up and set out to paralyze my dream. It spoke loud and clear. First of all, fear told me, it wouldn't work. Secondly, fear asked, "where are you going to get the money from?" I had sleepless nights and even frightening dreams at times. I felt sick to my stomach because I knew this couldn't happen in my own power. But when I went to church that Sunday morning and Pastor Bam unleashed that POWERFUL Word, a light bulb came on. I knew *my turn had come*! I had to take a leap of faith and put into action the words I had been speaking out of my mouth. I knew I couldn't sit on it any longer, I had to move quickly.

I stepped out, and a few months later I opened my own business. I'm so excited to say in April 2018 it will be five years. All glory to God! I have always had a dream to have my own business and to be my own boss. And today, I am so thankful that Pastor Bam was led by the Spirit of God to deliver the message, "Dream the Impossible Dream." I am a testimony of how one person can impact the life of another person in such a way that causes radical change. So, I say to you Mom, keep doing what you do and lives will continue to change. Love you!"

- From a Sister Dreaming of OWNING her own BUSINESS

"What a heartfelt honor to have been asked by my spiritual Mother *(the BEST on the planet)* to provide a testimonial for her powerful and transformational book, *It's Your Turn NOW!* God connected us at a women's conference over ten years ago in 2008, but little did I know how God would use this mighty woman of God to play a crucial and necessary role in my life. Only God knows the fullness of her impact. Although I have experienced success, she has inspired and challenged me to live out my true purpose. Specifically, I understood I had a passion and calling on my life as an author and speaker but Pastor Alma empowered me to step out and do what I was called to do by the help of our awesome God. Although this book had not yet been birthed at the time, she understood, *"It's Your Turn NOW!"*

It's impossible to be in her presence for any length of time or listen to one of her countless messages and not want more of God. Pastor Alma said "YES" to God many years ago, and her "YES" has allowed Him to use her in a unique and special way. Her hunger for God is immediately recognizable, contagious, and undeniable. One of the greatest points I've taken from this book has to do with the knowledge Pastor Bam has concerning her purpose. The importance of purpose is evident in the story she tells about God healing her from asthma as a ten-month-old baby and simultaneously endowing her with a special anointing. It lends credence to the importance of the God-given purpose God has for each of us. I can articulate with bold confidence and without reservation, I have been encouraged to challenge my doubts and confront my fears. And I believe like me, this book will encourage you too, to take the necessary and decisive steps to fulfill your God-given purpose because, *It's Your Turn NOW!"*

– From a Sister in Need of a CHALLENGE

"I've been a member of Spirit and Truth World Outreach Church since July 2003. One Sunday morning, in early February 2011, Senior Pastor Edwin Bamberg and Co-Pastor Alma Bamberg, announced we were relocating our church services to a hotel. That announcement rocked my world. I know it really doesn't matter where you worship, but I didn't want to worship God on a regular basis in a hotel. I faced a real dilemma! But I'm so grateful today, that I made the most important decision of my

Christian walk and life when I decided to follow my pastors to the hotel."

"First of all, I knew it was the right decision when I was no longer torn in my spirit and experienced complete peace. Even more importantly, we had only been having worship services in the hotel for one month when *I received a devastating positive result from my annual mammogram.* After completing all the secondary testing, I was scheduled to have a lumpectomy on Thursday, March 10, 2011.

The day before the lumpectomy, March 9, 2011, I went to Bible study. Prior to that night, I had not mentioned my health condition to any of my church members including my pastors. Just before Bible Study began I was able to speak with our Co-Pastor Alma. She took the news like a soldier which refortified my faith. Not only that, but just before the benediction Co-Pastor called me to the altar for prayer. She anointed me with oil and prayed the most powerful prayer of healing. The Holy Spirit overshadowed me with the healing power of God. I remember falling under that power sick, but I got up healed. From that moment to this one, I have been CANCER FREE. And on March 9, 2018, it will be seven (7) years, and I'm still FREE of CANCER! Thank you, Jesus! I am so glad I made the right destiny decision for my spiritual covering, growth, and my life by following my spiritual leaders to that hotel."

- From a Sister in Need of HEALING

"If I could say anything about Pastor Alma Bamberg, it would be that she has truly been a GREAT inspiration to me spiritually, emotionally, and naturally. When I first became a part of her ministry I was a broken vessel. At the time I was lost, searching, trying to find my way. I really didn't know what God's purpose or plan was for my life. I really didn't think I had a purpose. Then God placed Pastor Alma in my life for a divine purpose. I can definitely say that she has made a great impact in my life. I am the person I am today because of her strong influence on my life. Believe me, it didn't happen overnight. She was patient with me, but diligent. She never gave up on me. She taught me that I am who God says I am, and that I am not defined by my position or circumstances. She taught me, if I would continue to trust and believe in God, everything I needed would follow. I am *FREE in my mind* today and *HAPPY about life*. I know it's my turn and It's My Turn Now!!! I want to thank you Pastor Alma for obeying God and helping me to become the woman I am today."

– From a Sister in Search of PURPOSE

"The summer of 1994 would be bitter, but it would be the sweetest in my life. The murder of my fourteen-year-old cousin, caused a searching in my heart to take place. Within a few weeks of his funeral services I wanted to go to church. I found myself returning to the only church I knew as a child. There was a pulling in my heart I couldn't explain at the time, but God was drawing me to Himself. As I walked through those doors, not dragged or coerced by anyone, just free willed, I would encounter the God of a woman named Evangelist Alma Bamberg.

The Encounter: "As he journeyed, he came near Damascus, and suddenly a light shone around him from Heaven." Acts 9:3 KJV

As I walked in, I noticed the church was packed and the people of God were filled with an anticipation to experience God. The anticipation was palpable. You could just sense that something was about to happen in that atmosphere. The preliminaries had taken place, but there was a part in the church service that was new to me. I hadn't been to church in so long; it was a "new thing." The next part of the service was called "Praise and Worship" and the praise and worship leader was none other than, respectfully, Sister Alma Bamberg. I remember her being such a classy, eloquent in speech, and just a naturally beautiful lady. The moment she opened her mouth to lead the congregation into praise and worship, I was in awe. I couldn't take my eyes off of her. I had never seen anything like it. I had heard people talk about God and what He could do, but I was literally encountering the presence of God through music and she was the vessel. When she sang, there wasn't just excitement, but the power of God was displayed. While singing she exhorted, spoke to our situations of the week, and invoked the presence of God. Through adoration to Him, worries disappeared, yolks were broken, spirits were healed, and liberty was the end result. Captives were set free and the enemy was slaughtered. Sister Bamberg, respectfully, would lead us into the presence of God to the point where our praise became undignified. Her well made up face, bouncy beautiful flowing hair, and white ephod was now misted with perspiration because of her exuberant, passionate, love and expression for her God in song and dance. She gave God all of her. She emptied herself before Him. I watched her surrender every gift and talent over to the Lord to minister to God's people. I remember after this encounter, I couldn't keep the experience and her, Sister Bamberg, this lady, this praise and worship leader to myself. The first person I told my encounter to was my blood sister. The best way I could explain Sister Bamberg's delivery that morning was that she was a beautiful puppet on a string and God was the puppet master. She used the whole pulpit to minister, to the right, the left, an arm up and a leg, a skip, hands raised, and a bowing before the King. When encountering her, I encountered God. I encountered Jesus. I sensed joy, love, peace and most of all, I saw such a bright, bright light that demanded and commanded to be acknowledged. There was no denying or ignoring this light. It was the light of God. I acknowledged that light that day and determined in my heart that I wanted what she had. I wanted the light that shined so bright in her and everything that came with it. I wanted Jesus!!! Just as Saul encountered a great light on the road of Damascus that changed his life, I encountered a great light in the vessel of God, Co-Pastor Alma Bamberg. I encountered Jesus and my life was about to change!!!

The Life: "Mark the perfect man, and behold the upright, for the end of that man is peace." Psalm 37:37

From that day till this day, for 23 years, my eyes have marked Co-Pastor Alma Bamberg. I've been able to mark her for this long span of time because "the Light", Jesus, was ever shinning in her brighter and brighter with different reflections just as seasons change. Like a diamond when cast in the light, the reflections are colorful, varied and endless. Diamonds are forever, solid and sturdy!!! These examples describe her displayed faith in her God. *Co-Pastor Alma's life is an encyclopedia filled with volumes of life's lessons lived out through the Word of God.* It was approximately 5-6 months of attending church irregularly that I gave my heart to God. *Why? Why did I give my heart to God? The reason I gave my heart to God was because I encountered a vessel prepared to lift God up in her being and life.* The Word of God states that if I be lifted up, I will draw all men unto myself. From where I sat, there wasn't an area in the life of Evangelist Alma that didn't reflect the light of God. Evangelist Alma was developed intellectually, emotionally, and relationally. She was developed in her self-image and womanhood. She displayed a confidence and boldness foreign to me. All of who she was, was foreign to me. She was married and they looked happy. This to, was foreign to me. Just as she ministered during praise and worship, preaching the Word of God, the two were identical, impactful, powerful and provoking. During praise and worship, her cry and a plea to God would be, "God we can't make it without you, and we need you!" These words burned in me, they were the sentiments of my heart too. I was so in love with God and I wanted all He had for me, but I wanted to give Him me too. *Evangelist Alma's invitation to Christ didn't just stop with "Jesus loves you and wants you!" She was unselfish to admonish hearers, "What I have, you can have, God gave it to me, and it can be yours too!" "It's your turn!"* Her statement heralds the statement of Jesus, "I've come that you may have life and that much more abundantly." Her life exemplified "The Life", her life hidden in Christ. This was "The Life", and I wanted it. It was simply mine for the asking."

- From a Sister Hungry for God

"In my life I had been misused, abused, called out of my name, overlooked, counted out, and forgotten about by those who said they loved me. What individuals did to me, I also did to myself. I was clueless as how to love myself and respect myself. The morning of that first encounter with Sister Bamberg, I had gotten out of a bed with a young man that I was shacking with in my mother's house. My actions were disrespectful. This young man who said he loved me, was abusive in every way; and later diagnosed as mentally ill. I kept the abuse a secret from everyone. I was embarrassed. I had learned to tolerate abusive relationships from the relationships around me. But now, I didn't want it, I wanted to be free!!! But I was afraid of him. Not to rush through the process of being physically free, in a nutshell, I almost didn't make it out. Towards the end of being totally free, I acquired scars around my wrist that are barely detectable now. I was raped, stalked on my job, invited by him to die with him by suicide and lastly, a gun pulled on me. The young man would try to discourage me from attending church, but I kept going, and going. I went to Sunday morning services, Women's Sunday school where Evangelist Bamberg would assist in teaching. I would go to Bible study where Pastor Edwin Bamberg would teach during the week and she would assist. I'll never forget the series *"Strongman's his name, what's his game"*. I learned so many principles that strengthened my resolve for change.

But, *it just wasn't my resolve that was strengthened, but my courage increased and fears toward this young man decreased.* I even boldly shared the Word of God with my boyfriend. He went to church with me one or two times but wanted no parts of it. I was challenged by the Word of God and the standard Evangelist Alma Bamberg lived and preached about as a disciple of Jesus Christ!!! "You have to be holy, your bodies don't belong to you!!!", she would say in a women's ministry she founded called *Sisters of Destiny*. The ministry was a safe place for women to mentor younger women regardless of age. I wanted to be holy! I didn't want to have sex and not be married. I wanted to only give myself to God; it was the right thing to do!!! It bothered me that I continued to be sexually active and a Christian. But as I continued to be taught and applied Romans 12:2, "And be not conformed to this world but be ye transformed by the renewing of your mind..." a change occurred in my life.

I'll never forget the night God set me free!!! All the Word, all the seeds sown, were about to yield a harvest of right decision making that would set me free to a life that I couldn't author nor imagine. The night of my senior prom blinders came off my eyes and courage flooded my heart. That night the young man was my date and at the end of the night I told him that we were breaking up and he needed to leave my mother's house. The next day, I packed his clothes and put him out. This was the summer of 1995. I went into the depths of God and enjoyed it!!! I was so free and happy. The fall of 1995 would prove to be even more exciting!!! There were many others who've had a profound impact on my life, but I have to say that because of being exposed to Co-Pastor *Alma's anointing, life of faith, and Christian convictions, as a babe in Christ I was totally ruined for a mediocre lifestyle in God in every area of my life.* As a result, I've excelled in every way.

After high school, I started college that summer and graduated as a registered nurse in 2002. While in college, I was a member and college Bible study leader with Campus Crusades for Christ. I accepted my call as a licensed evangelist-missionary, traveling to East Asia and to the Dominican Republic. My services and gifts were shared with many. While serving the Lord, He blessed me with my "kingdom partner", man of God, and Minister of the Gospel. Remember that conviction of being "holy" that was etched in my heart in those early days while encountering Co-Pastor Alma? That conviction and standard to God lasted from the age of 19 years old to my turning 35 years old. *I knew not another man until my wedding night. That conviction alone saved me so many pitfalls that were strategically set to derail me.* To God be the glory for a woman who didn't think teaching God's standard of "Holiness" was a thing of the past. Our family is blessed and flourishing under the leadership of Pastor Edwin Bamberg and Co-Pastor Alma Bamberg. Yes, God brought me full circle with this "Dominion Couple."

- From a Sister who was MISUSED, ABUSED, and FORGOTTEN

"I have to speak about the "mother spirit" of Co-Pastor Alma Bamberg. Instead of being a mother to natural children, God arranged for her to be a mother to her local church and to the nations. I am totally in awe and filled with amazement for the mothering spirit she possesses. She handles and nurtures each spiritual child delicately, skillfully and when necessary firmly in godliness. I would venture to say that I've witnessed and experienced a motherly hand and I can confidently say that it's better than some mothers who have birthed natural children. Being a spiritual mother carries a great weight to it, and in some cases, have proven to be far weightier than being a natural mother. As a spiritual mother, more intercession is needed, more counsel is needed, and more accountability is needed. As she goes with God, we're invited to go with her. I promise you, if you decide to follow, you'll also go as I did, to places in God that are deeper, higher, and further than you imagined. She's qualified to take you there! She's been faithful, steadfast, and continues to abound in God!"

- From a Sister Needing a SPIRITUAL MOTHER

"I am a better person because Pastor Alma is in my life. She inspires me to pursue the greatness that God put in me. She is my Pastor, my spiritual Mother and my friend. Pastor Alma is a lady, she dresses superbly, has an extremely positive attitude and is always smiling and inspires me to do the same. She knows who she is and who she belongs to – Jesus! She walks tall, shoulders back, and head lifted. She exemplifies confidence and inspires confidence in me. Pastor Alma allows me to see a "modern day" example of holy living. There are many examples in the Bible, but she is *living proof* I can observe right NOW. She's proof that the Word of God works. She's proof that prayer really works. And she's proof that I can depend on God. Pastor Alma strengthens my resolve to live a life of integrity for God – when no one is watching and I'm all alone. Pastor Alma continues to help and support me during the pain and disappointment of a non-fulfilling marriage. She prays for me when I get sick and her prayers are effective. I'm healed every time she prays for me. I never doubt her love for me. My self-esteem has risen, my desire to pray and be in the presence of God has increased and my desire to use the gifts God has given me has increased. Watching her minister and operate in her prophetic gift is awe-inspiring. When I was a little girl, my initial inspiration for the *Spiritual Gifts* in operation came from a now deceased minister, who had an evangelistic healing and deliverance ministry. And now, I am learning from Pastor Alma. In all these years of joining church after church, I am finally home – where I am growing and maturing in the things of God. I thank God for causing my path to cross the path of Pastor Alma Gordon Bamberg!"

- From a Sister Needing PROOF THAT GOD CAN BE TRUSTED

"Pastor Alma has been a motivation in my life by always being a role model. Ways that she has encouraged me to TAKE MY TURN is by simply being an example. She has been a model of a godly wife, a fearless leader, a warring intercessor, a loyal friend and overall a woman who no doubt let's Jesus shine through her. Pastor Alma's ministry has forced me out of my comfort zone and place of stagnation. She has without a doubt given me tools to expand in regards to the things of the Lord. Her words are always so positively encouraging and stretches me to get all that God has for me and do all that God has called me to do. I am where I am in my life today, because of her help. I am forever grateful that God has allowed Pastor Alma to be my spiritual Mama!"

- From a Sister Needed to be Forced out of her COMFORT ZONE & STAGNATION

"Pastor Alma Gordon Bamberg is a gem of rare form and value. Of her many gifts and talents, I am so thankful for her unique vision. I will never forget one day when she pulled me aside, and cupped my face in her hands, the way she does. She looked me in the eye, and said, "I see you." Those three powerful words were so important to me. As a woman, wife, mother, sister, daughter, manager, and all the many hats I wear day-to-day, I was losing sight of myself. When Pastor Alma took the time to stop, see me, and provide wise counsel, she helped me to see me. She helped me to take a step back, prioritize, and make sure that "self" was on my list. Thank you, Pastor Alma. Love you, Always."

- From a Sister needing to PRIORITIZE HERSELF

Dedication

Blood Sisters

Six years ago, when God placed this book in my heart, I knew I wanted to dedicate it to the three beautiful women that taught me the true meaning of sisterhood, my blood sisters, *Cheryl Genise, Debra Remonia,* and *Ursula Yvette.* We were blessed to grow up as PKs. For those of you who don't know what PKs are, its preacher's kids. In our case, it also meant pastor's kids. I pray this book serves as an echo of the heart of God for each of you. He knows the paths you've traveled. He's allowed you to go in the direction you've gone in and He's using everything you've experienced for such a time as this. The good, the bad and the ugly, all of it has prepared you for such a time as this. You are the Esthers of today and someone's waiting on you to take your turn!

The Bible speaks of a man by the name of Zelophehad in Numbers chapter twenty-seven who had five daughters and no sons. Their father died and the law said they were not eligible to receive what was rightfully theirs just because they were females. They petitioned the spiritual leadership of that day and asked a very poignant question: *"Why should the name of our father be removed from his family because he had no son? Give to us a possession (land) among our father's brothers. So, Moses brought their case before the Lord. Then the Lord said to Moses, "The request of the daughters of Zelophehad is justified. You shall certainly give them a possession as an inheritance among their father's brothers, and you shall transfer their father's inheritance to them. Further, you shall say to the Israelites, if a man dies and has no son, you shall transfer his inheritance to his daughter."* [1]

Cheryl Genise, Debra Remonia, and Ursula Yvette, when I read this passage of scripture it reminds me of us, four daughters born to a man who had no sons. Of course, we thank God, at the time of this writing, our father and mother are still both alive and we rejoice daily for the blessing of them in our lives. But just because our father didn't have any sons doesn't mean we're NOT entitled to our inheritance! Both our parents have imparted a solid godly heritage in us and *it's our time NOW* to possess what God says is ours! God has transferred our father's godly inheritance to us!

> ...just because our father didn't have any sons doesn't mean we're NOT entitled to our inheritance!

I pray this book will encourage each of you to boldly *take your turn* without hesitation or reservation! Fulfill the call of God on your life and make no apologies for it. Our father and mother have given us a great name and godly heritage that will live on in each of us. It's your Turn NOW, Gordon Girls. TAKE IT!

Sisters in Christ

Secondly, this book is dedicated to *my sisters in Christ all over the world.* To my sister who's unprepared and needs to know that a turn is waiting on her; to my sister who's in the middle of the process of preparing for her turn; and finally, to my sister who's prepared, ready and stepping forward to take the turn she so desperately waited for.

> Always in a mode of getting ready and never being ready causes weariness and an inward desire to give up.

It is very important to realize you must come to a point when you are finally ready to move forward. Always in a mode of getting ready and never being ready causes weariness and an inward desire to give up. The Bible says hope put on hold will make you sick. Proverbs 13:12 says, *"The hope that is deferred, is the fainting of the heart, but when the desire cometh, it is as a tree of life."* (Geneva Bible) To know you've done what is required to be prepared gives life. I pray this book will empower you along the journey we call life by providing you with a proven process of preparation that was so masterfully exemplified in the life of Esther.

Sisters Behind Bars

Last, but certainly not least, this book is dedicated to my dear sisters locked up behind prison bars. To my sisters waiting in line for your turn to arrive, I write this book with you in mind. More specifically, I dedicate this book to you, Jane *(Not the actual name)*. Thank you for writing me that all so special letter written from your jail cell asking me to be your spiritual mentor. Your letter had a profound impact on my life and further compelled me to write this book. Jane expressed her love for reading and sharing the knowledge she'd gained with others but was grossly aware that she needed someone to mentor her. I'll never forget the statement in her letter that arrested my attention. She said, *"I'm teaching others, but who's teaching me?"* WOW!

Her request caused my water to break and induced the labor pains that informed me that I was ready to deliver this book. I vividly remember leaving that county jail feeling her pain and cry for help. Heavy of heart, I cried out to God and asked: "How can I provide mentorship to my young sister and others like her?" As I drove over the causeway, disturbed in my soul, intrusive thoughts from the Spirit of God flooded my mind. I knew I had to do something and I had to do it now! You see, I had brought Jane one of my ministry compact disc (CD) entitled, "You're not What Happened to You." Not remembering inmates could only receive letters and paperback books that had been sent through the mail, I was unable to share what I believe would have been a word in due season and refreshment to her soul.

By the time I arrived at my destination, thirty minutes later, I knew I had to translate my audible messages into books and get them into that jail. I had to WRITE! I thought, "Why not mentor her and others like her through books?" My turn had come. I had to give birth! I could no longer hide this book in my heart. So, to you, my dear Jane and others who share your current situation, regardless of how things might look today, I want you to know you don't have to forfeit your turn. Whatever you've done that has caused you to be locked up behind prison bars doesn't have to deny you of your turn.

> Whatever you've done that has caused you to be locked up behind prison bars doesn't have to deny you of your turn.

Please don't think I'm only referring to my sisters in a physical jail or behind prison walls. No, imprisonment is not just limited to physical bars but also mental, emotional and psychological bars. Incarceration of the mind is just as restricting if not more and is often the result of negative situations that occur in your life. Perhaps many times, tragic and horrific conditions occur during childhood that's no fault of your own. The enemy of your soul knows if he can start a mental pattern of thinking at an early age it becomes a stronghold. He positions a grip on your soul and with great strength refuses to let go without a fight. If you can come to understand the power you possess when you come into relationship with Jesus Christ, you will realize the spiritual weapons you have in Him are far greater than anything Satan can use against you. The Bible is clear. The weapons we use to fight with are not physical but are spiritual weapons that are mighty through God. These weapons are so strong that they will demolish every stronghold the enemy uses to try to bind your mind with thoughts that are contrary to God's plan and will for your life. *"The weapons of our warfare are not physical [weapons of flesh and blood]. Our weapons are divinely powerful for the destruction of fortresses. We are destroying sophisticated arguments and every exalted and proud thing that sets itself up against the [true] knowledge of God, and we are taking every thought and purpose captive to the obedience of Christ"* (2 Corinthians 10:4-5).

I pray this book provides you with a strategic plan of action that will help prepare you for the great life God has already prepared for you. Jeremiah 29:11 (NLT) says, *"For I know the plans I have for you," says the Lord. "They are plans for good and not for disaster, to give you a future and a hope."* As you sit there, perhaps, all alone with no hope of a brighter future and for some, no knowledge of when you might be free to physically join your family and loved ones in what we call the free world, I believe this book will breathe fresh hope and possibility back into your life. For others of you, it is my desire that when you are free to do what you want to do, go where you want to go and have what you want to have, this book in some way will have prepared you for what lies ahead.

Most of all, as a result of reading this book, I pray that the Spirit of God will infuse you with the faith necessary to understand that taking your turn can occur right now! You don't have to wait for your situation or circumstances to change before you change. True transformation takes place first in your mind. If you can change your mind, it won't be long before everything about you changes too. So, I strongly encourage you to get prepared because *It's Your Turn NOW!*

Table of Contents

Testimonials iv
Foreword..xxvi

Section I: MY PERSONAL SPIRITUAL RETREAT 1
   Chapter 1:   Mental Detox 1
   Chapter 2:   An Unshakable Resolve......... 9

Section II: THE PREPARED WOMAN.................................16
   Chapter 3:   Esther's Story..17

Section III: THE PROCESS OF PREPARATION................24
   Chapter 4:   The Bath of Bitterness..27
   Chapter 5:   Sweet Spices and Perfumes 41
   Chapter 6:   Help! I'm Stuck and I Want to Get Out.................49

Section IV: THE PRINCIPLES OF PREPARATION...........59
   Chapter 7:   My Purpose..65
   Chapter 8:   My Plan..79
   Chapter 9:   My Period..93
   Chapter 10: My People..107
   Chapter 11: My Profession...119
   Chapter 12: My Position...133
   Chapter 13: My Price 139
   Chapter 14: My Promotion 147

Section V: THE PRAYER OF PREPARATION 157
   Chapter 15: God's Ultimate Plan for You...............................157
   Chapter 16: My Prayer for You...162

Notes..166
Acknowledgements...168
About the Author 171

FOREWORD

Bishop Rosie S. O'Neal

It's not often that you find someone who is as kind as she is determined or as sweet as she is strong, but there are not many people like Alma "Bam" Bamberg. For years, I have been blessed by her friendship and by the anointing on her life to stand, speak and shift the atmosphere. I have watched her stand boldly in faith during difficult times and continue to bless all of those to whom she ministered. I have also seen her soar like an eagle without losing her passion for Jesus or the well-being of the people of God. She has helped countless people to overcome adverse situations and then use those situations as opportunities to advance! Her personal testimony shared in this book will convince you of the faithfulness of God and the certainty of the victory that belongs to you! Bam's praise and prayer life gives her prophetic authority to unlock the potential within others, launching them into their "now" season.

It's Your Turn Now is designed to empower you with spiritual and practical tools to step firmly and confidently into the season of God's best for your life. I believe that we all understand that really big shifts require an adherence to a proven process to ensure our success. "Bam" shows us not just what God wants to do but guides us through that process toward the promotion that He has for our lives. The thought provoking questions at the end of the chapters will challenge you to take a deeper look inside yourself and hear what the Lord is saying to you! I want to encourage you to read it intentionally, then allow the Holy Spirit to rebuild any broken places and hear Him say, *"It's Your Turn Now!"*

SECTION I

My Personal Spiritual Retreat

CHAPTER 1

Mental Detox

At the end of each year, I purposely set aside time to seek direction and insight for the upcoming year. I call it my *"Personal Spiritual Retreat"*. On December 30, 2010, I checked into a hotel room and began my end of the year mental process of detoxification. I look forward to an annual practice of cleansing my mind from any toxic effects of the outgoing year and preparing for the incoming year with a sense of clarity of thought and peace of mind. Needing to eliminate the old before beginning the new is very important in making sure the "new" that God wants to do in my life for the incoming year, is not contaminated by the "old" from the previous year. I'm sure you would agree with me that

> Oftentimes, we detox our bodies, but we forget to detox our minds.

IT'S YOUR TURN NOW!

"life" has a way of introducing mental toxins designed to destroy your peace of mind. Oftentimes, we detox our bodies, but we forget to detox our minds.

As a child, my parents instilled in me the importance of extended designated times of prayer, fasting, seeking the face of God, and being still in His presence. We call it times of "consecration". Consecrations are prioritized times spent with God over everything and everyone with the expressed purpose of developing a sensitivity to the voice of God to receive clarity and direction from Him. It's a time of denying fleshly desires to receive greater spiritual sensitivity through prayer and fasting. We often sing the lyrics of the song *"Fill Me Up"* by Casey J that says, "I want more," but are we willing to do what's necessary to receive more? One of the benefits I enjoy during times of consecration is the privilege of private conversations with God, during which many questions are asked and answers are received. The main questions, as I enter a new year have always centered around, *"Who am I NOW? and What am I called to do NOW?"* The operative word is NOW. I want to know and understand God's plan for my life at that particular season of my life.

> "Be alert, be present. I'm (God) about to do something brand-new. It's bursting out! Don't you see it? There it is!"

My sister, I'm sure you're aware that we are constantly changing, not only in dress sizes but in our personal interests and desires as well as in what God desires for us. There are times in all of our lives when God desires to do something new in and through us. He is in a constant state of changing us into the image of His Dear Son. I love what the prophet Isaiah said: *"Remember ye not the former things, neither consider the things of old. Behold, I will do a new thing; now it shall spring forth; shall ye not know it? I will even make a way in the wilderness, and rivers in the desert"*. Isaiah 43:18-19 (KJV) The message Bible makes it even clearer, *"Be alert, be present. I'm about to do something brand-new. It's bursting out! Don't you see it? There it is!"*

How May I Serve YOU?

As my 2010 personal retreat came to an end, I knew I had experienced the undeniable presence of God. I received many precious revelations during my time alone with Him; revelations that I will forever cherish. The greatest is the premise that helped to inspire the writing of this book when God spoke ever so gently, yet it was indelibly etched in my inner most being. He said, *"Alma, It's not only your time, but it's your TURN"*. Of course, I had heard that statement before, but that day, it resonated in my spirit and became a driving force that I knew was not a fleeting thought.

As I pondered the statement for clarity and understanding, I was reminded of a particular fabric store I often frequented. Sewing and designing has been a love and passion of mine since a child

> For someone who's reading this book and you feel like life is cutting you, God wants you to know, it's only because you've been selected.

IT'S YOUR TURN NOW!

and spending time at the local fabric store continues to be a great pastime for me. For those of you who are unfamiliar with how fabric is purchased, the process begins with a fabric selection that's usually stored on cardboard bolts. Each bolt contains yards of fabric. After selections are made, the desired yardage is cut by a store representative. Let me take a moment and speak to someone who's reading this book and you feel like life is cutting you, God wants you to know, it's only because you've been selected.

Usually, there are customers waiting in line to have their fabric cut, therefore you're not served immediately. When there's a line, the next step in the process is to retrieve a number from a dispenser, much like you would in a deli, and then you must wait your TURN. When your number is called, you proceed to the cutting table. The person cutting the fabric most generally says, *"Next"* and then *"How may I SERVE you?"* This is the point where further clarity came to me. God spoke in a series of short statements, *"Alma, you've got next! You are next in line! Your number is up! It's your TURN to be served!"* I thought to myself, *"served?"* The response was, "YES! Served." Not in the sense that others would serve me as a waiter would serve a table in a restaurant, but rather, you, Alma, are the entrée, the main course God has prepared to serve to others. I realized at that moment that God was notifying me that I was "done" with some things and now it was time to move forward into what He had *ALL-ready PREPARED* for me. What are you done with? Are you ready to move forward? WOW! To be served? Powerful!

ALMA GORDON BAMBERG

Progressively Transformed

In that cozy hotel room, all alone with the lover of my soul, I wrote his personal Word to me. This is the way it was given to me: *"Alma, you are a prepared entrée that's now ready to be served to others! The fruit from the previous seasons of your life is ripe, as in a meal having been prepared and ready to serve hungry people from what I have given to you. You have completed the necessary preparation that was required to cultivate your fruit, and today, you are ready for the next level of glory in Me."* The life of a person who has made a decision to follow Christ is in a constant state of movement from one level of glory and faith to another level of glory and faith. Next level glory includes next level exposure. The Spirit of God continued to speak, *"It's time for your fruit to be exposed to different people, places, and experiences. This exposure is not necessarily for your benefit alone but more importantly for the benefit of others."*

Whenever I am impressed in my spirit with a word from God, I know it must always line up with scripture. I searched the scriptures for confirmation and before long, I found myself reading 2 Corinthians 3:18(KJV) which says, *"But we all, with open face beholding as in a glass the glory of the Lord, are changed into the same image from glory to glory, even as by the Spirit of the Lord."* The Amplified Bible of that same scripture reference states, *"And we all, with unveiled face, continually seeing as in a mirror the glory of the Lord, are progressively being transformed into His*

IT'S YOUR TURN NOW!

image from [one degree of] glory to [even more] glory, which comes from the Lord, [who is] the Spirit." God's plan for our lives is a glorious progressive transformation, one degree at a time of becoming more like him.

I looked at my trusted *spiritual retreat* companion, my lap top computer, and typed what I knew was God's directional word for my life for the incoming year. Little did I know that word would be the prevailing word to provide the foundation for this book and still breathes life into me today. Here I am, eight years later to date after receiving that word. I know without a doubt, *it's my Turn, Now* to serve YOU the word that was spoken to me then. The number eight represents *new beginnings* and I believe God is giving not only me a fresh start, but you too!

God's plan for our lives is that we are in a perpetual state of producing fruit, and that the fruit we produce, remains and bring glory and honor to Him. The book of John 15:8,16 (KJV) says, *"Herein is my Father glorified, that ye bear much fruit; so, shall ye be my disciples. Ye have not chosen me, but I have chosen you, and ordained you, that ye should go and bring forth fruit, and that your fruit should remain: that whatsoever ye shall ask of the Father in my name, he may give it you."* What are you producing now? Your life today is a product of what you've sown in your past. So be careful what you sow today, it's an indicator of what you will reap tomorrow.

> ...be careful what you sow today, it's an indicator of what you will reap tomorrow.

ALMA GORDON BAMBERG

It is no accident that you are reading this book. I believe that Word, spoken to me in that hotel room, on that brisk December morning, was *not* just for me! I believe God is in the process of forcing you out of a place of complacency and beyond your comfort zone. He is requiring of you something different, something more and something new!

CHAPTER 2

An Unshakable Resolve

The Moment is NOW!

You might be wondering, what is it my turn for? *It's your turn* to succeed at the call of God on your life. *It's your turn* to prosper, to lead, to rule, and to have dominion! *It's your turn* to be above only and not beneath! *It's your turn* to walk in divine health, uncommon favor, and overwhelming peace! *It's your turn* to write that book, start that business, or whatever you've been waiting for the right time to do. *It's your turn* to be on the cutting competitive edge.

> Don't you want to be where God is and not where He was? Don't you want to do what God is doing NOW and not what He did last time?

Don't you want to be where God is and not where He was? Don't you want to do what God is doing NOW and not what He did last time? This is your moment to be and do all that God has created you to be and do. The moment is now!

I challenge you today to make a bold declaration: *It's "MY" turn, NOW!* Let me inform you up front, that I will often ask you throughout this book to make statements about yourself that may

IT'S YOUR TURN NOW!

or may not be apparent in your life at the moment. But if you continue to say in faith what God says, it won't be long before you start believing what you've been saying. Before you know it, whatever you've said and believed will show up in your life. The book of Hebrews chapter eleven says something very important about our faith. It says faith is "NOW". That means you are in current possession of what you believe you receive. Your faith is the substance of the things you're hoping for right now. It is also the evidence of what is not apparent to your physical senses but it's real, waiting on you to make the transfer from heavenly places. Ephesians 1:3 says, God has already blessed us with all spiritual blessings in heavenly places in Christ. In other words, if your blessing hasn't manifested in the natural yet, be assured it has been set aside for you in the spiritual realm if you can only believe. Your faith is what enables you to make the transfer from the spiritual realm into the physical realm.

Your statement of faith is a necessary part of the transfer process. So, right now, I want you to make a personal confession of your faith. Say it out aloud with me, *"It's My Turn NOW!"* Say it with passion! *"It's My Turn NOW!"* Say it as if you've been waiting for your turn a long time! *"It's My Turn NOW!!!!!!!!!"* Please understand this statement is not a self-righteous, braggadocios statement, but rather, it's a statement of confidence. The confidence you possess in God's desire for you to succeed in life! It's a statement of faith! Today I agree with you that *it's YOUR Turn, and it's YOUR turn, Right NOW!*

ALMA GORDON BAMBERG

An Unshakable Resolve to "TAKE" Your Turn

An unshakable resolve to "TAKE" your turn is the kind of mentality that reminds me of a time when I was a kid waiting my turn in a game of kickball. After what seemed like eternity, it was finally my turn to kick. I would inevitably shout, "It's my turn!" and if anyone tried to take my turn, I would say, "NO, you can't get in front of me. It's my turn!" I refused to allow anyone to take my turn! That's exactly the mentality we must possess when things that are rightfully ours have been taken from us. I don't know what has been taken from you; maybe it's your self-worth, confidence, joy, or peace. Maybe it's a relationship; perhaps drugs have taken your child; or your health has been taken by a debilitating disease; or maybe it's your finances to bankruptcy. I can't speak for you; you've got to identify it yourself. But what I can say is, whatever it is, it's time to TAKE IT BACK! I've come to realize, when it's time to take your possessions back, especially from Satan, you can't allow yourself to be passive. You've got to take it by force! Taking it by force requires a mindset that says, by any means necessary I will not be denied my turn!

Perhaps you've found yourself waiting for what seems like an eternity to have your turn in the game of life and just when it's your turn, something or someone always seems to get in your way. These are the times when you must demonstrate an unshakable resolve to take your turn. This book is

> ...no one can stop you, but you.

designed to help you do just that! The truth of the matter is no one can stop you but you.

What are "You" going to "DO?"

It is important to affirm what you believe by making scriptural based confessions, but there comes a time when you've got to DO something! I'd like to call your attention to a story in the fifth chapter of the book of John. There was a man who had been lying by the pool of Bethesda. For thirty-eight years he waited for someone to help him get into the pool at just the right moment to receive his healing. Jesus showed up knowing how long the man had been waiting and asked him a question. *"Would you like to get well?" He replied, "I can't, sir, for I have no one to put me into the pool when the water bubbles up. Someone else always gets there ahead of me." Jesus told him, "Stand up, pick up your mat, and walk!" Instantly, the man was healed!"* John 5:6-9 (NLT)

I want you to note, Jesus never addressed the man's complaint about needing help from someone else to get well. This man had to come to the realization that what he needed wasn't the mercy and benevolence of others. The help he needed was always inside of him. The reason he was in that condition was based on his actions and his actions alone. How did I come to that conclusion? Later on, in the chapter we see where Jesus finds the man in the temple and tells him, *"Now you are well; so, stop sinning, or something even worse may happen to you"* John 5:14 (NLT). The understood subject is YOU. The man's inability to walk was rooted in previous sins he had committed. The power to change his life was under his control all the time.

Oftentimes, we too, sit around waiting for someone one else to do for us what only we can do for ourselves. You know the old adage, "excuses are a dime a dozen." It's time to take control of our lives and do for ourselves what we've been waiting on someone else to do for us. This book is written to help you come to the realization that what you need is not the mercy or benevolence of others. God has already put "in" you what you need to get up and out of your stupor and "TAKE" what's rightfully yours. Someone is waiting on you to "Take" your turn"! It is my greatest desire that you, my dear sister will come to realize, it's YOUR TURN, NOW! So, let's make it happen. I feel like I need to quote Nike, "Just DO IT"!

> ...what you need is not the mercy or benevolence of others... God has already put "in" you what you need to get up and out of your stupor and "TAKE" what's rightfully yours.

Daily Application Required

At the end of each chapter, I'd like to encourage you to take time to reflect and think about the action steps you will take to employ what you've learned. I pray you are provoked to act now, don't delay! In the words of Benjamin Franklin, *"You may delay, but time will not."* Please use this section as a road map to guide you through to your personal predestined path of purposeful living.

IT'S YOUR TURN NOW!

You will be given opportunities as you read for self-reflections.

> Please be honest when answering each question and make sure your answers reflect where you are NOW and not where you were or would like to be.

There are questions for you to answer that will facilitate self-awareness, clarity, and understanding. Please be honest when answering each question and make sure your answers reflect where you are NOW and not where you were or would like to be. As you examine your life, create a workable plan that will prepare you for your turn.

I admonish you to boldly forge ahead with an assurance that you're not alone. God is always with you and ready to help. His Word says, He'll never leave you or forsake you (Hebrews 13:5); He sent the Holy Spirit to live inside of your heart as a helper if you only invite Him in (John 14:26); and please know, you have a sister in me. I'm standing in the gap for you and praying with confidence knowing because we've asked according to God's will for your life, He hears us and we have the petitions that we've requested of Him (1 John 5:14).

You must consciously make a daily decision to govern your life by proven principles found in the Word of God. As you study and apply them, get ready to set in motion scriptural laws that will cause accelerated opportunities and success in your life. It is with great humility that I challenge you to apply them today! It is also important to understand, in order to arrive at your predestined place of purpose, you must be willing to do the work! Remember, this is a personal journey and it's your turn NOW to make it happen. So, let's get started. Enjoy the journey!

SECTION II

The Prepared Woman

This book examines the life of an orphan girl by the name of Esther. It provides a glimpse into the mentality of a prepared woman. She understood it was her turn to make a difference in the life of someone other than herself. She understood to forfeit her turn would result in the death of a nation of people whose hope and future depended on her selfless act of obedience. Esther was a woman who understood it was her turn. The reason she understood it was her turn was because she was willing to do what was necessary to prepare herself. Section II is devoted to telling Esther's story.

CHAPTER 3

Esther's Story

Esther's story is found in the Old Testament Scriptures of the Bible. Her story was so important that an entire book has been dedicated to the telling of it. She is one of two females to have a book in the Bible named in their honor. For thousands of years her story has been preserved and passed down from generation to generation. Her story gives us undeniable proof of the providential care of Jehovah God for the Jewish nation of Israel. Esther, a helpless orphan girl adopted by her cousin Mordecai, found herself plunged into the midst of a highly competitive beauty contest that ultimately led her to the royal position as Queen of Persia. Let's take a look at how her story unfolds.

Royal Position VACANT

"In those days when King Ahasuerus who was also called Xerxes sat on the throne of his kingdom, which was in Shushan the citadel, that in the third year of his reign he made a feast for all his officials and servants—the powers of Persia and Media, the nobles, and the princes of the provinces being before him— when he showed the riches of his glorious kingdom and the splendor of

IT'S YOUR TURN NOW!

his excellent majesty for many days, one hundred and eighty days in all." (Esther 1:2-4 NKJV)

On the seventh day, when the heart of the king was merry with wine, he commanded ... seven eunuchs ..., to bring Queen Vashti before the king, wearing her royal crown, in order to show her beauty to the people and the officials, for she was beautiful to behold. But Queen Vashti refused to come at the king's command ...; therefore, the king was furious, and his anger burned within him." (Esther 1:10-12 NKJV)

A recommendation was made to the king: *"If it pleases the king, let a royal decree go out from him, and let it be recorded in the laws of the Persians and the Medes, so that it will not be altered, that Vashti shall come no more before King Ahasuerus; and let the king give her royal position to another who is better than she.* (Esther 1:19 NKJV)

Then the king's servants who attended him said: "Let beautiful young virgins be sought for the king; and let the king appoint officers in all the provinces of his kingdom, that they may gather all the beautiful young virgins to Shushan the citadel, into the women's quarters, under the custody of Hegai the king's eunuch, custodian of the women. And let beauty preparations be given them. Then let the young woman who pleases the king be queen instead of Vashti. This thing pleased the king, and he did so." (Esther 2:2-4 NKJV)

Favor Shown to the Undercover Jewish Girl

"So, it was, when the king's command and decree were heard, and when many young women were gathered at Shushan the citadel, under the custody of Hegai, that Esther also was taken to the king's palace, into the care of Hegai the custodian of the women. Now the young woman pleased him, and she obtained his favor; so he readily gave beauty preparations to her, besides her allowance. Then seven choice maidservants were provided for her from the king's palace, and he moved her and her maidservants to the best place in the house of the women. Esther had not revealed her people or family, for Mordecai had charged her not to reveal it. (Esther 2:8-10 NKJV)

Each young woman's turn came to go in to King Ahasuerus after she had completed twelve

> "Thus prepared, each young woman's turn came to go in to the King..."

months' preparation, according to the regulations for the women, for thus were the days of their preparation apportioned: six months with oil of myrrh, and six months with perfumes and preparations for beautifying women. Thus prepared, each young woman went to the king, and she was given whatever she desired to take with her from the women's quarters to the king's palace. In the evening she went, and in the morning, she returned to the second house of the women... She would not go in to the king again unless the king delighted in her and called for her by name. (Esther 2:12-13; 14 NKJV)

IT'S YOUR TURN NOW!

Now when the turn came for Esther ... to go in to the king, she requested nothing but what Hegai the king's eunuch, the custodian of the women, advised. And Esther obtained favor in the sight of all who saw her. So, Esther was taken to King Ahasuerus, into his royal palace, in the tenth month, ..., in the seventh year of his reign. The king loved Esther more than all the other women, and she obtained grace and favor in his sight more than all the virgins; so, he set the royal crown upon her head and made her queen instead of Vashti." (Esther 2:15-17 NKJV)

Opportunity Cloaked in a Problem

King Ahasuerus, *"promoted Haman son of Hammedatha the Agagite over all the other nobles, making him the most powerful official in the empire. All the king's officials would bow down before Haman to show him respect whenever he passed by...But Mordecai refused to bow down or show him respect.* (Esther 3:1-2 NLT) *When Haman saw that Mordecai would not bow down or show him respect, he was filled with rage. He had learned of Mordecai's nationality, so he decided it was not enough to lay hands on Mordecai alone. Instead, he looked for a way to destroy all the Jews throughout the entire empire.* (Esther 3:5-6 NLT) *When Mordecai learned about all that had been done, he tore his clothes, put on burlap and ashes, and went out into the city, crying with a loud and bitter wail.* (Esther 4:1 NLT)

When Queen Esther's maids and eunuchs came and told her about Mordecai, she was deeply distressed... (Esther 4:1a NTL)

...She ordered one of her servants to go to Mordecai and find out what was troubling him and why he was in mourning. (Esther 4:5b NLT) *Mordecai told him the whole story, Mordecai gave the servant a copy of the decree issued in Susa that called for the death of all Jews. He told the servant to show it to Esther and explain the situation to her. He also...directed her to go to the king to beg for mercy and plead for her people."* (Esther 4:7-8 NLT)

Problems Reveal Purpose

Mordecai gives Esther a stern warning and declares her fate if she fails to bring relief and rescue her people from their perishing predicament. *"Do not imagine that you in the king's palace can escape any more than all the Jews. For if you remain silent at this time, liberation and rescue will arise for the Jews from another place, and you and your father's house will perish [since you did not help when you had the chance]. And who knows whether you have attained royalty for such a time as this [and for this very purpose]?"* (Esther 4:13-14 AMP) *Then Esther sent this reply to Mordecai: "Go and gather together all the Jews of Susa and fast for me. Do not eat or drink for three days, night or day. My maids and I will do the same. And then, though it is against the law, I will go in to see the king. If I must die, I must die."*

How is it, that Esther could make a bold statement like that? What was it, that had prepared her to take that kind of stand and boldly take her turn? Esther had finally discovered her purpose! It was hiding in her problem. She had finally found not only a reason

IT'S YOUR TURN NOW!

to live but a reason to die! She was fully persuaded that speaking on behalf of the Jewish nations was what she was born to do. She had a resolve: "I either do this or I die". No, she didn't start off with that kind of resolution, but as she simply obeyed the one who had the charge over her, be it Mordecai or those over the harems, her courageous faith developed along the way. She had come to a place of preparation that had produced an audacious tenacity to take a stand. What would produce such a resolute mindset? What did she know?

As I carefully examined Esther's story trying to answer those questions myself, I uncovered eight fundamental principles that I will share in Section III of this book. Esther's story was a testament to these principles and were, what I believe, some of the essential keys to her courageous response.

> Could it be that God wanted women to have a proven example of what it would take for a woman to properly rise to a position of power and authority?

I believe what Esther knew is so critical for us to know, that God made sure her story was preserved for thousands of years. What she knew guaranteed her promotion and rise to the highest position of authority for a woman in her day. Could it be that Esther's story was preserved to teach women how to prepare themselves to become their best and highest expression of themselves? Could it be that God wanted women to have a proven example of what it would take for a woman to properly rise to a position of power and authority? I believe YOU are that woman, a woman of power and authority.

ALMA GORDON BAMBERG

Esther's story was written and preserved for you. She courageously took her turn and she showed us how. Now it's your turn. What will you do? How will your story read and what will you show others?

SECTION III

Process of Preparation

"Each young woman's turn came to go in to King Ahasuerus after she had completed twelve months' **preparation**, *according to the regulations for the women, for thus were the days of their* **preparation** *apportioned: six months with oil of myrrh, and six months with perfumes and* **preparations** *for beautifying women.* [13] *Thus* **prepared**, *each young woman went to the king..."* (Esther 2:12-13a NKJV)

It's imperative to note how many times a derivative of the word prepare is used in Esther 2:12-13a NKJV. Four times, the word preparation or prepared is used. Anytime a word is repeatedly used in scripture, we should take time to dig deeper to see what lesson God is teaching us. One very important lesson Esther's story teaches is the process of being prepared. Why is this lesson important? Because one of the worse things that I believe could ever happen to an individual is to be given an opportunity or promotion and not be prepared for it. Preparation is a state of being ready. Of course, I'm fully aware that no one is 100% prepared as it relates to skill level or even confidence all the time, but there is a place of readiness that's within a person's power and ability that causes him or her to avoid missed opportunities. Warning: Please don't wait until an opportunity presents itself and then decide, "Well, I guess I'd better get prepared" when you could have already done the necessary work to be prepared. It'll be too late.

You must prepare now for promotions God has predestined for you. I hear you my sister, "What if I don't know what to prepare for? How do I prepare for a promotion I'm not aware exists?" Great questions!

First of all, I don't want you to think only in terms of jobs and money when I speak of preparing for a promotion. Promotions are opportunities for greater. Promotions can be opportunities to be a better person, elevations in a mindset or belief systems, or just living at a higher quality of life. Let me assure you promotion exists for all of us. Irrespective of where a person is in life, what a person has, or what a person does, greater increase is possible in some area or the other.

Secondly, what do you know about yourself? What godly desires do you currently have? What is the last set of instructions spoken to you either in your spirit or by an authority figure in your life? Start there and do that. You don't have to know how everything is going to work out. The Bible says, it starts with a blade of corn, then an ear of corn and finally, the full ear in the corn. I can hear Apostle I. V. Hilliard saying, "God gives you more on the way than He does before you get started". Just get started.

> "God gives you more on the way than He does before you get started".
> *- Bishop I.V. Hilliard*

IT'S YOUR TURN NOW!

Oftentimes, God speaks to us through those we are submitted to. This is one of the ways to demonstrate to God you can be trusted. Once you demonstrate you can be trusted with the last step or instruction He gave you, then He will reveal the next step. The Bible says *"The Lord directs the steps of the godly. He delights in every detail of their lives"* (Psalms 37:23 NTL). I know, many of us would rather pick up the pace and run, but God says He's concerned about guiding each step we take as we submit. It's a walk of faith, not a run of faith based on 2 Corinthians 5:7 KJV. Preparation involves a series of steps often referred to as a process and processes takes time.

Section III is devoted to the preparation process each young virgin had to undergo in order to have her turn with the king. It gives a detailed account of the first twelve months of not only Esther's preparation process, but every woman in the harem. Each woman was prescribed predetermined protocols to follow. Preparing to see the king didn't occur overnight. Again, it was a process. And might I remind you, we too, are preparing to go before our king, King Jesus. It too, requires a process; a process we all must go through.

This section sets the stage for a greater understanding of the preparation process we must submit to in order to have an audience with our king. It provides spiritual implications and life lessons that are relevant for today as you prepare to take your turn.

CHAPTER 4

The Bath of Bitterness

*"Now when every maid's turn was come to go in to king Ahasuerus, after that she had been Twelve months, according to the manner of the women, (for so were the days of their purifications accomplished, to wit, six months with **oil of myrrh**, and six months with sweet odours, and with other things for the purifying of the women;)"* (Esther 2:12 KJV)

It's Bath Time

Soaking in a warm bubble bath with scented candles clustering my Jacuzzi with underwater jets massaging and invigorating my body, listening to my favorite soft smooth music is a great way to spend the evening. When I think about that scene, it makes me want to close down my computer and leave my writing for a later time. But because I'm in a flow, I'd better wait until later for that. I'm not sure if that scene is what Esther's six months of bathing in oils of myrrh was like. But what I do know, is that the bath of myrrh, was a necessary part of the process in order to have an audience with the king.

In ancient civilizations, myrrh was very valuable. We commonly hear it referenced during the Christmas season as one of the gifts presented to the infant Jesus by the wise men. It is one of the ingredients found in the sacred anointing oil used in so many religious services and ceremonies. Even today, there are many medicinal purposes as well as cosmetic uses for myrrh. As I studied the properties and benefits of myrrh I came across an interesting property of myrrh that I believe can bring clarity and insight as to why this type of oil was used as the oil of choice for preparation. *"The word "myrrh" comes from "murr," which means "bitter" in Arabic, probably referring to its bitter taste."* [1] The word "bitter" denotes a sharp, unpleasant taste. The things you will endure to prepare yourself for your turn, will without doubt, include distasteful circumstances.

You can expect bitter times as a part of God's preparation process for the Believer. Peter calls it fiery trials. I Peter 4:12-13 (NLT) says, *"...don't be surprised at the fiery trials you are going through, as if something strange were happening to you. Instead, be very glad—for these trials make you partners with Christ in His suffering, so that you will have the wonderful joy of seeing His glory when it is revealed to all the world".*

The trial comes to reveal the quality of your faith.

The Amplified Bible of that verse says, trials come *"to test the quality of your faith"*. The Message Bible calls it *"... a spiritual refining process"*.

There's no doubt about it, bitter experiences, or as Peter would call it, fiery trials are required to release the anointing in your life. I know we all desire the anointing, but are we willing to go through the bitter situations and the distasteful circumstances of life? If you expect to be prepared when your turn comes, you should also expect to be bathed in bitterness.

Taking a bath is different from taking a shower. Usually in a shower you are standing and the water is running on and off your body. But a bath, allows you to sit down and be submerged in the water, that's how fiery trials are. They don't just hit you and then run off. No, they take the position of rest and linger around turning good into bad much like your bath water. When you first get in the bathtub the water is clean, but by the time you get out, the clean water has turned murky. Have you ever felt like you were submerged in a test that never wanted to end? Perhaps, you felt like you were drowning? When you do, always remember the purpose for the trial. The trial didn't come to take you out or under but rather to take you up. The trial comes to reveal the quality of your faith.

Difficult divorces, unexpected health challenges, unforeseen layoffs, vanishing finances, death of a child, they all are a part of life. And life happens to us all, good and bad, bitter and sweet. Knowing how to respond in good times and when life is sweet is not usually a problem. But how should you respond when times are bad and things are bitter? What will your attitude be? James 1:2b (NLT) gives insight as to what the proper attitude should be. He said," *...consider it an opportunity for great joy."* When you respond to bitter situations that way, life becomes a gym of faith, working out and building faith muscles to the point where your faith is completely developed and you are spiritually mature.

It's Working Together for Your Good

God has a way of taking a bitter situation and working it together for your good. One of my favorite scriptures is Romans 8:28: *"And we know that all things work together for good to them that love God, to them who are the called according to his purpose."* When you encounter a bitter situation, you've got to know something, not guess, but know. What should you know? First of all, there must be a complete confidence in God and that somehow, someway, some good is coming out of this! You must be assured that "ALL" things – not just good things, but also the bitter things of life are working together for your good too.

I like to compare this passage of scripture with the process of making a cake and its most common ingredients. The most important ingredient is flour, but the flour alone doesn't make the cake. There are other basic ingredients required to have a finished product. For example, you have to add eggs, butter, sugar, and extract. Even after adding all the basic ingredients in the bowl the cake is not complete. I don't know anyone who would look at those ingredients in a bowl unstirred and commence to eat it. Why? Because the flour alone is dry. The eggs alone are slimy. The butter alone is oily. The extract alone is bitter. Now, the sugar alone is sweet to taste but it's only a small percentage of the ingredients. The majority of the ingredients are distasteful in its uncooked state if ingested individually. But I dare you to stir it all together. Before the cake is done, your children will fight over the remaining batter in the bowl or spoon. It hasn't been put into the oven yet, but because you mixed it together, what was once distasteful is now pleasing to the taste.

That's exactly how the bitter situations of life are. You must take all the painful distasteful experiences of your life and mix them together with the Word of God, the Spirit of God, the power of God, and your faith in God and watch Him work it together for your good! You've got to learn how not to look at your problems and your pain in isolation. When you only look at the pain of what happened to you and not consider why it happened, you miss the lesson it came to teach.

> When you only look at the pain of what happened to you and not consider why it happened, you miss the lesson it came to teach.

Let me take a moment to encourage someone who's gone through a difficult divorce; an embarrassing bankruptcy; a never-ending battle with a wayward child; a painful death of a loved one; or a discouraging health challenge and you've been looking at your situation in isolation. I challenge you to mix it together with all the other events of your life and add in the grace and mercy of God. I'm sure you'll be able to find some good in it. And may I take a moment to encourage that single mother, who was left to raise all of those children alone and you thought you weren't going to make it. You thought you would lose your mind. And yes, what you experienced is real, and you thought you weren't going to come through that. But look at you now. You're still here! You're still standing!!

Heated Temperatures

The apostle Peter in his first book to the New Testament Church warns them that the trials that they would face would be "fiery." In other words, their trials would be on fire, intense and extremely hot. I don't really get along very well with the heat. I'm not a fan of hot places. Currently, I live in Texas and in the summer months it can be extremely hot. I can't speak for anyone else, but I'm really grateful for the person who invented the air conditioner. I don't like heat, it makes me very uncomfortable! So, it is, in the spiritual realm, the preparation process is not always a very comfortable place either. You will often experience extreme heat, but God knows a little spiritual heat won't hurt you. He has pre-set your trial to the exact temperature for your growth and development. Like the cake, after the whipped batter is poured into the desired shaped cake pan, the baker presets the temperature and waits until the desired temperature is reached. He knows it's the heat at the proper temperature for the right amount of time that causes the cake to rise. The baker follows the recipe putting the batter in the pre-heated oven trusting the heat to do what it was designed to do within the allotted time.

Just like the cake that goes into the oven and undergoes extreme temperatures to become everything the baker intended for it to become, you too, must undergo extreme fiery trials to become all that God intends for you to become. Without the heat, the batter will never reach its full potential and neither will you. You might be in the oven of life right now, but know this, you're rising! You're coming up and out of that trial and rising to that glorious place God has predestined only for you. Whether you realize it or not, just like the cake, you being able to withstand the heat is the only thing that will cause promotion in your life.

Faith Under Pressure

Some of us are impatient. Well, let me speak for myself. I don't always enjoy the waiting process. Maybe it's more accurate to say, I never enjoy the waiting process. I must admit there have been times when I've taken the cake out of the oven too soon and instead of it rising, my cake caved in. And so, it is with many Christians when it comes to getting out of our fiery faith tests. We are impatient. We don't want to stay in the heated faith process; consequently, we fall down, undeveloped and incomplete. James, the brother of Jesus, gave instructions as to how to handle a heated faith test when we have an urge to bailout before the process is completed. He said, *"Consider it a sheer gift, friends, when tests and challenges come at you from all sides. You know that under pressure, your faith-life is forced into the open and shows its true*

IT'S YOUR TURN NOW!

colors. So, don't try to get out of anything prematurely. Let it do its work so you become mature and well-developed, not deficient in any way." (James 1:3-5 The Message Bible)

How do I know when I'm Ready?

How do you know if you are ready to be served to others? Let's go back to the cake illustration. The fact that the cake is rising, is not a true indicator alone that the cake is ready to be eaten. So how do you know if a cake is truly done? Well, I'm from Louisiana and the way we tested a cake back in the day to determine if it was done or not may not be the way the top chefs do it today, but for the sake of my illustration I will share it.

So, what we did was to give the cake the old "broom" test. You might be saying, "Did I hear you say, "broom"? Yes, I did say broom and it was actually the broom we swept the floor with. The cake was slowly removed from the oven just in case it wasn't completely done and set ever so gently on the kitchen counter. I would pull a straw from the opposite end of the broom, the part that had not touched the floor and slide it delicately into the cake. The process was repeated several times. If at any time when the straw was carefully examined by holding it up to the light and there were signs of cake batter left on the straw, the cake was not done. Back into the oven it went.

What does this have to do with whether or not you are ready to be served to others? If the same ungodly behavior that was a part of your everyday life before you went through your fiery trial is still a part of your everyday life after you come out of your fiery trial, you're not ready! I hate to inform you, but you didn't pass the readiness test! You must repeat the test! There is no social promotion in the spiritual realm. If you're still cussing everybody out every time you don't get your way, you're not ready! If you're popping your neck and raising your hand saying, "speak to the hand," you're not ready! I'd like to encourage you to stay in the spiritual oven a little longer. God preset the temperature that's required for best results and He knows exactly how long to keep you in that heated oven. He won't let you burn up. He's after that sweet aroma that emanates from a purified soul. He knows the exact temperature necessary to burn away the impurities lodged in a contaminated soul.

You know the cake is done when you stick that straw in the cake and it comes out clean. The only way you and I can be made clean is by the washing of the water by the Word of God. (Ephesians 5:26) That's the purpose of reading and studying the Bible. The Word of God is a sanctifier. It separates the pure from the impure; the godly from the ungodly; the truth from a lie; the good from the evil and the holy from the unholy. Please hear me, God is not looking for a perfect person but He is looking for a clean heart. The Psalmist said, *"Create in me a clean heart, O God; and renew a right spirit within me"*. (Psalm 51:10) Do you have the "right spirit"? The Message Bible says, *"Soak me in*

IT'S YOUR TURN NOW!

your laundry and I'll come out clean, scrub me and I'll have a snow-white life."

As we come to the close of this chapter, you know as well as I do, every cake that comes out the oven isn't a pretty cake. Some cakes come out leaning and lopsided. They may be a little flawed but the true test of a good cake is based on the taste, not the looks. I've tasted a many of cakes that were absolutely gorgeous and weren't half as good as they looked. On the other hand, I've seen a cake or two that wasn't so pretty, but it sure tasted good. You don't have to be perfect. God uses flawed people. But an unregenerate heart, He can't use.

> God uses flawed people... But an unregenerate heart, He can't use.

Regeneration is all about change. That's what the preparation process is all about. It's about God changing us into the image and likeness of Christ. You cannot clean up yourself without the help of God. If you could, I'm sure you would have by now. The power of God to prepare us to serve others is available right NOW! All you have to do is ask Him like David did in the fifty-first division of the book of Psalms. Repeat his words with me – *"Create in me a clean heart, O God; and renew a right spirit within me"*. God will use the bitter situation or season of your life that the enemy thought was going to *distract* you, *discourage* you, and *deny* you of your turn, to PREPARE you for the greatest season of *grace* and *favor* you've ever seen!

ALMA GORDON BAMBERG

Don't be Surprised

The Apostle Peter warned the New Testament believers about the trials they would face. He didn't want the difficulty they would experience to catch them off guard and unprepared. He wanted them to know, trials were a necessary part of their faith process. He told them, *"Beloved, do not be surprised at the fiery ordeal which is taking place to test you [that is, to test the quality of your faith], as though something strange or unusual were happening to you"* (1 Peter 4:12a Amplified Version). The latter part of that scripture from the Message Bible describes the fiery trials as *"...a spiritual refining process, with glory just around the corner."* That's good news! Something good is coming out of your trial! The benefit of going through a fiery trial is God's glory on and in your life.

God is ultimately after His glory being revealed in your life. He desires for you to be an effective witness for Jesus Christ. Therefore, you're constantly being changed into the image of His Dear Son through the things you suffer. That is what this bath of bitterness is all about. Look at what the Bible says Jesus learned through the things He suffered. *"In the days of His earthly life, Jesus offered up both [specific] petitions and [urgent] supplications [for that which He needed] with fervent crying and tears to the One who was [always] able to save Him from death, and He was heard because of His reverent submission toward God [His sinlessness and His unfailing determination to do the Father's will]. Although He was a Son [who had never been disobedient to*

IT'S YOUR TURN NOW!

the Father], He learned [active, special] obedience through what He suffered." Hebrews 5:7-8(AMP) Listen my sister, you might find yourself bathing in a bath of bitterness, but know this, God is preparing you for something greater!

IT'S YOUR TURN NOW TO WORK ON YOU

<u>Self-Reflection Exercise:</u>

Ask yourself –

1. Have I ever felt like I was drowning in a test that never seemed to end? What was it?
   _____
   _____

2. How should I respond when my circumstances are bitter and distasteful? What will be my attitude?
   _____
   _____

3. When I encounter a bitter situation what should I know?_____
   _____

4. What is God wanting to teach me through the things I suffer? _____
   _____
   _____

5. What is God preparing me to do as a result of the suffering in my life? _____
   _____

CHAPTER 5

Sweet Spices and Perfumes

"Now when it was each young woman's turn to go before King Ahasuerus, after the end of her twelve months under the regulations for the women—for the days of their beautification were completed as follows: six months with oil of myrrh and six months with [sweet] **spices and perfumes** *and the beauty preparations for women"*

— (Esther 2:12 AMP)

Aromatherapy

Thank God, the preparation treatment God prescribes for the Believer doesn't end with the bath of bitterness, and neither did Esther's purification process. The Bible is clear that the last six months of Esther's purification treatment included "perfumes and cosmetics." Thinking back over a previous spa experience, sweet aromas and pleasant smells were a vital part of setting a calming and relaxing environment. The distinct fragrances were a part of what was called, aromatherapy and is known to have medicinal benefits.

IT'S YOUR TURN NOW!

Aromatherapy or essential oils therapy is using a plant's aroma-producing oils (essential oils) to treat disease. Essential oils are taken from a plant's flowers, leaves, stalks, bark, rind, or roots. The oils are mixed with another substance (such as oil, alcohol, or lotion) and then put on the skin, sprayed in the air, or inhaled. You can also massage the oils into the skin or pour them into bath water. Practitioners of aromatherapy believe that fragrances in the oils stimulate nerves in the nose. Those nerves send impulses to the part of the brain that controls memory and emotion. Depending on the type of oil, the result on the body may be calming or stimulating. [2]

The first six months of purification was designed to extract impurities from the bodies of the young ladies in an effort to prepare them for a night with the king. Removing contaminates did not complete the process. Fragrances were added to their bodies that were not only therapeutic but pleasing to the senses producing a calming and stimulating response. These sweet odors added an aroma to the skin that would be attractive to the king.

Prayer-Roma Therapy

Prayer has a fragrance too. The aroma of prayer is attractive to God and gets His attention. It goes up into the heavens as a sweet-smelling savor to Him. The book of Revelations compares prayer to fragrant incense: *"And when He had taken the scroll, the four living creatures and the twenty-four elders fell down before the Lamb (Christ), each one holding a harp and golden bowls full of fragrant incense, which are the prayers of the saints (God's people)."* (Revelations 5:8 AMP) *"And another angel came and stood at the altar, having a golden censer; and there was given unto him much incense, that he should offer it with the prayers of all saints upon the golden altar which was before the throne. And the smoke of the incense, which came with the prayers of the saints, ascended up before God out of the angel's hand."* (Revelations 8:3-4 KJV)

There is an unforgettable aroma that emanates from the life of a person who respects the practice of prayer. You don't have to announce you are a prayer warrior, others will know it when you show up.

> There is an unforgettable aroma that emanates from the life a person who respects the practice of prayer.

Signature Perfume

I recall a recent encounter I had with two young girls who attends my church that taught me a lesson about the potency of a fragrance. I had been working at the church in my office all day and as I began to wrap up to leave, I couldn't locate my sun glasses. I remembered I had left them in another office on the opposite end of the building. I was in a hurry and didn't want to get sidetracked by those attending various rehearsals. So, I asked my husband if he would drive me around to the front of the building so I could run in, without being noticed to retrieve my sunglasses. I made it to the business office, slipped in, certain that I had avoided everyone. As I opened the door to leave, I turned to lock it, and out of nowhere, two young girls who were there for dance rehearsal came running up to me saying, "Dear, Dear, we knew you were here, we could smell your perfume."

I thought I had made a clean get away but my perfume gave away my presence. The girls had been around me long enough to recognize my signature fragrance and made the connection. I thought just because no one saw me, no one would know I was there. But the scent from my perfume announced my presence even without me saying a word. And that is exactly what happens to a person who establishes regular times of communing with God through prayer. Prayer acts as a magnet to the blessings of God. God will put an anointing on your life that will attract others to you. That explains why people are drawn to you and they don't know why. Not only will people be drawn to you but the blessings of the Lord will track you down as well. Those young girls came running up behind me and overtook me before I was aware of their presence. It reminded me of the Scripture that says, *"And all these blessings shall come on thee, and overtake thee…"*. (Deuteronomy 28:2)

ALMA GORDON BAMBERG

God's Perspective on Beauty

I think it is important to highlight where true beauty comes from. Let's take a look at what the Word of God says about meekness. Psalms 149:4 KJV says, *"For the Lord taketh pleasure in his people: he will beautify the meek with salvation."* 1 Peter 3:3-5 (NLT) gives a clear warning to women about lasting beauty: *"Don't be concerned about the outward beauty of fancy hairstyles, expensive jewelry, or beautiful clothes. You should clothe yourselves instead with the beauty that comes from within, the unfading beauty of a gentle and quiet spirit, which is so precious to God. This is how the holy women of old made themselves beautiful..."*. This text is not encouraging women to neglect their outward appearance, but rather, it emphasizes the disproportionate amount of attention given to temporary things like clothes, jewelry and hairstyles as opposed to things that have an eternal value.

What God values most, is a woman with a decked-out spirit. He values a woman who has learned how to manage her soul in such a way that she doesn't allow her emotions to dictate her responses. I'm sure we've all seen a beautiful woman on the outside but as soon as she opened her mouth or we observed her mannerism or the rude way in which she dealt with others, we quickly concluded, she's not so beautiful after all. Because of her negative disposition her beauty quickly faded away.

God makes a commanding connection between beauty and meekness. Meekness in short has to do with humility and is the basis for God's perspective on beauty. Meekness is not weakness.

IT'S YOUR TURN NOW!

Meekness is having strength, but not allowing strength to have you. Meekness means you are in total control of your temperament. When the Bible refers to *"the beauty that comes from within" and a "meek and quiet spirit"*, could it be that what God is really after is a proper attitude? Are you aware that your attitude is much like a lingering perfume? It can be pleasant or unpleasant and you don't have to open your mouth to know which is which. Is God pleased with your attitude? Could you be emitting a foul smelly odor from your attitude that's displeasing to God? Do you have a quiet and meek spirit? Do you need an attitude adjustment? If so, I'm here to tell you, it's your turn now to step into the steam bath of prayer and allow your spiritual pores to open as the water of God's Word envelopes you and the Holy Spirit gently pulls out the impurities that seek to clog your soul.

IT'S YOUR TURN NOW TO WORK ON YOU

Self-Reflection Exercise:

Ask yourself –

1. How is my attitude like a lingering perfume? _____ _____

2. When the Bible refers to "the beauty that comes from within" and a "meek and quiet spirit", what is He really after? _____ _____

3. Is God pleased with my attitude? _____

4. If "NO", Why am I emitting a foul smelly odor with my attitude that's displeasing to Him? _____

5. What does a quiet and meek spirit look like on me? _____ _____ _____

6. What can I do to adjust my attitude to better please God? _____ _____

IT'S YOUR TURN NOW!

CHAPTER 6

Help! I'm Stuck and I Want to Get Out!

The "Esther Fast"

When Esther didn't know how to come before the king, God gave her a plan. Esther's instructions to Mordecai was, *"Go, gather all the Jews who are present in Shushan, and fast for me; neither eat nor drink for three days, night or day. My maids and I will fast likewise..."* (Esther 4:15-16). As a result of this time of fasting, God gave Esther a plan on how to fulfill her purpose. I know the "Daniel Fast" is popular today, eating only fruits and vegetables. But Esther said no, I don't want a "Daniel Fast" proclaimed on my behalf. I need everybody to go on the "Esther Fast" because my life is on the line!" She told Mordecai to tell all the Jews not to eat or drink anything for three days and three nights as they sought the face of God on her behalf. She was desperate!

IT'S YOUR TURN NOW!

I'm Stuck and I CAN'T Get Out

Esther knew if God didn't give her a plan, the law demanded her death. It reminded me of a desperate situation I found myself in one Sunday morning as I prepared to leave my home. I accidentally closed two of my fingers in the trunk of my car. I opened the trunk, removed the items I was retrieving and pushed the button to close the trunk door. As I walked along the side of the car, I unconsciously place my hand on the car in such a way that the trunk door caught two of my fingers. As the door closed down, the automatic suction mechanism locked the trunk down on my hand. I began to feel an excruciating pain! Unable to free myself, I began yelling my husband's name hoping he would hear my cry for help. It was a cry of desperation because I wasn't sure he could hear me.

You see, generally on Sunday mornings prior to church, he's upstairs behind closed doors possibly with ear phones in his ears meditating or putting the finishing touches on his sermon. My garage door was down and there was no way for me to open it or even move. I was stuck and I couldn't get out! I wondered, could any of my neighbors hear my cry of desperation? At a certain point, I didn't care who freed me, I just wanted to get out. Thank God, my husband eventually heard me, came and freed my fingers from the trunk. I didn't lose any fingers and I was fine after I finally calmed down.

Strangest thing about that ordeal, just before going to the trunk of my car, I was thinking about how we, as women often feel stuck in abusive relationships, dead end jobs, and life in general. I remembered thinking about the commercial where the elderly lady falls and says, "Help, I've fallen and I can't get up." Do you remember that commercial? My initial thought was, that should be a sub-title in my book because that's exactly what I want this book to do. I want it to help women who have fallen and need help getting up. But then I recalled thinking, no, that's not the right wording. Not even ten minutes later, I go into my garage and my fingers get stuck in the trunk of my car.

I'm Stuck and I WANT to Get Out

Immediately after I regained my composure and realized not one of my bones was broken or fractured, I began thanking God and giving Him all the glory and praise. I remembered the Psalm where David said *"Many are the afflictions of the righteous: but the Lord delivereth him out of them all. He keepeth all his bones: not one of them is broken"* Psalm 34: 19-20 (KJV). Praise the Lord! God didn't allow any of my fingers to be broken. I could easily move them as I had before. And even the initial indented marks from the closure of the trunk's lid had all disappeared in less than 30 minutes. I knew without a shadow of doubt that that experience had come to teach me something about what it takes to get unstuck. That's why I chose to title this subsection, "I'm Stuck and I Want to Get Out." Since I paid such a

Lesson #1:
You can't get out by yourself.

IT'S YOUR TURN NOW!

dear price to learn these lessons, I must share them with you:

First of all, if you are stuck and you want to get out – *You can't get out by yourself.* At some point in life you'll need help outside of yourself.

It doesn't matter what your educational background is, your family history, your economic status, or social class. Your age, race, or nationality doesn't matter either. It doesn't matter who you are, there will come a day when you will need help. As I stood there looking for a way to free myself from the trunk, I realized I couldn't reach the switch to open the garage door; I couldn't reach the back of the truck to hit the release button; nor could I reach the front car door to hit that release button. I was in an awkward position on the left side of the car with my right hand stuck. I couldn't get out by myself, I needed someone to help me.

> **Lesson #2:**
> **You must ask for help.**

Secondly, I learned, if you are stuck and want to get out – *You must ask for help.* You've got to open your mouth.

When my fingers were stuck in the trunk of the car the only way someone was going to come to my rescue was if I opened my mouth and cried out for help. This is a major problem for a lot of us. I think if we are honest with ourselves, many times the root of the problem is pride. The implication of pride usually has to do with being arrogant and conceited. But pride is also independence. We think we should be able to handle everything on our own or

> **Lesson #3:**
> **You must ask persistently until help arrives.**

else there's something wrong with us. But I'm here to tell you *there is nothing wrong with asking for help.* Really, there's something wrong when you don't, and just maybe, it's PRIDE.

Thirdly, if you are stuck and you want to get out – *You must ask persistently until help arrives.*

Asking for help may not be your problem, but you've made up in your mind, "I'm not going to keep asking. If they wanted to help me they would have helped me by now!" WOW! What is that attitude all about? Please understand, life is happening to everybody. I'm sure the person you asked would love to help you, otherwise, you wouldn't have asked them. Did you ever think, just maybe they forgot and you needed to remind them? When my fingers were stuck in that trunk, I refused to stop screaming my husband's name until he showed up. If you need help, don't stop until you get what you need. If the first person you ask can't help you, find somebody else.

Next, if you are stuck and you want to get out – *You can't be choosy about who helps you.*

> **Lesson #4:**
> **You can't be choosy about who helps you.**

IT'S YOUR TURN NOW!

There was a point when my fingers were stuck that I began to wonder if my neighbor could hear my screams or perhaps someone walking in the neighborhood. You see, I wasn't 100% sure my husband could hear me and would come to my rescue. Sometimes the very person you were counting on will not be the one to help you. Don't be surprised who God puts in your life to help you. Sometimes it's the most unlikely person. So never discount anyone. You can't afford to be picky. When I wanted to get out, I didn't care who opened the trunk. They could have been black or white, rich or poor, educated or illiterate, young or old. I didn't care. JUST GET ME OUT!

The fifth lesson I learned, if you are stuck and you want to get out – *Getting out has to be important to you before it's important to someone else.*

> **Lesson #5:**
> Getting out has to be important to you before it's important to someone else.

When I called out my husband's name, I called it with a sense of urgency. He knew the way I called his name that time, wasn't the usual way I called his name. There was something about the tone of my voice, the piercing of the screams and the constant shouting of his name over and over and over that arrested his attention and caused him to move with the same level of intensity that was evident in my voice. Later on, he told me, when he heard my cry he got up so fast running down the stairs toward my voice, he knew he skipped at least five steps trying to get to me. What am I saying? If it's not important to you, how do you expect it to be important to someone else? In the words of Bishop T.D. Jakes, "How bad do YOU want it?" You determine how fast others respond to you. People move to the beat of your drum beat. You set the tempo.

And finally, I learned, if you are stuck and GOD gets you out – *He can remove all signs of the trauma you incurred from being stuck.*

> **Lesson #6:**
> If you are stuck and GOD gets you out, He can remove all signs of the trauma you incurred from being stuck.

There was no evidence left on my fingers that they had been closed in the trunk of a car. When I say no evidence, I mean not one bruise. The only thing I had left was a TESTIMONY! Hallelujah! And get this, it was less than 30 minutes after that ordeal, that I went right back to the trunk of the car, put my things in and went on to my Sisters Ablaze Life Class. And today, I can say, I'm cautious when closing the trunk of a car but I have no fear. I've chosen to use that experience as a teacher and not allow it to be a thief robbing me of my peace of mind. Excuse me, but I feel like shouting! Hallelujah!

God is the only one who can free you from past incarcerations of life and wipe away not only the pain of your past but He gets rid of the evidence so that no one can ever accuse you of it again, not even yourself! And then He removes the fear of it so that you can

IT'S YOUR TURN NOW!

go right back to the place where you experienced pain, rejection, hurt, abuse, and failure and boldly try it again. Yes, my sister, it's your turn to try it again!

Rescue Call

Maybe you, like me or Esther, have found yourself in a desperate position. If you would cry out to God in your distress, you can be assured that He hears you and will rescue you. God's Word confirms this over and over. Let me name just a few Biblical references of God's desire to rescue you. *"In my distress I called upon the Lord, and cried to my God: and he did hear my voice out of his temple, and my cry did enter into his ears"* (2 Samuel 22:7 KJV). *"In my distress I called upon the Lord, and cried unto my God: he heard my voice out of his temple, and my cry came before him, even into his ears"* (Psalms 18:6 KJV). *"The righteous cry, and the Lord heareth, and delivereth them out of all their troubles"* (Psalms 34:17 KJV). *"Then they cry unto the Lord in their trouble, and he saveth them out of their distresses"* (Psalms 107:19 KJV). *"Then they cry unto the Lord in their trouble, and he bringeth them out of their distresses"* (Psalms 107:28 KJV). It sounds like God is waiting to hear the cries of the distressed and is ready to deliver them from all of their troubles.

I understood getting my finger stuck in that trunk was more than a lesson, it was a physical experience. I had an opportunity to feel what it feels like to be STUCK in a situation and unable to get out without the help of someone else. At that point, I knew I had to complete this book. I felt a sense of urgency. I realized some woman's life is depending on me rescuing her as she reads this book!

Just like I needed someone to hear my cry and rescue me from that trunk of my car, perhaps you are "that woman" whose wondering, does anybody hear me? Does anybody see that I need to be rescued? I left that experience with not only a greater ability to sympathize with women or anyone who's stuck, but also to empathize with them. Yes, I've been in situations where I've felt stuck before, but none compared to that experience. The pain was great but the shear fear and extreme anxiety I felt about not being able to get out was beyond anything I have ever felt in the natural.

Just like I was in trouble and in need of someone to intervene on my behalf, women are in trouble and in need of God's intervention on their behalf. But you, my sister, must participate in His plan to rescue you. I believe with all my heart, God is looking for women who are desperate for Him! Women who desperately desire to fulfill the plans of God in the earth to the point where they are willing to prioritize His plans and purposes over their personal wants, desires and plans. My sister, it's time to boldly come to God in a cry of desperation knowing He will free you from any and everything that has kept you bound. He's waiting on you. It's all up to you. Do you want to get out?

IT'S YOUR TURN NOW TO WORK ON YOU

Self-Reflection Exercise:

Ask yourself –

1. What situation am I stuck in? _____
   _____

2. What are the devastating effects if I don't ask for help? _____
   _____
   _____

3. Who has God already provided to help me that I'm overlooking? _____
   _____

4. What am I doing to express my desire for help?
   _____
   _____
   _____

5. How can I use my fearful experience as a teacher and not a thief?
   _____
   _____
   _____

SECTION IV

Principles of Preparation

Principles Defined

This section is designed to stimulate your faith to live a principle driven life. You might ask, what are principles? Principles are laws that affect the way a person or thing functions. They are foundational truths that govern a person's belief system and behavior. Merriam-Webster defines a principle as a "code of conduct." So, why is principle living so important? Living by principles provide stability. They are constant, they do not change. Facts can change, but not principles. Living by principles produces consistency and predictability, thereby eliminating a whole lot of guess work. Principles have been tested and proven, so you know it works. Living by principles guarantees success over time.

This section is about preparing yourself for promotion. It really doesn't matter what type of promotion or advancement it is, these principles are a necessary part of the preparation process. If you want to excel in any area of life, understanding and applying these principles are key.

IT'S YOUR TURN NOW!

Eight Preparation Principles Exemplified in Esther's Life

This section will address eight principles exemplified in the life of Esther. These principles were the essential keys that prepared her to take a stand and boldly take her turn.

1) She discovered her *purpose*;
2) She refused to move forward without a *plan* from God;
3) She understood that there was a set *period* of time to fulfill her purpose;
4) She identified the *people* God placed in her life to help her fulfill her assignments and ultimately her purpose;
5) She realized her *position* wasn't just about outward beauty, but about changing legislation that would affect a nation;
6) She was willing to pay the *price* to fulfill her purpose, which ultimately resulted in her promotion. And
7) As a result of Esther applying all these principles in her life, it ultimately produced *promotion* for her to the highest position of influence, for a woman, in the Persian Empire.

I call these Principles of Preparation. These principles

> If you consistently apply these principles to your life, I'm convinced they will prepare you to face and maximize your most daunting God-given opportunities with courage, boldness and assurance!

were crucial keys that guaranteed proper preparation for Esther's promotion. They unlocked a door of opportunity that positioned her to use her powerful influence to positively affect an entire nation. I believe these principles hold the key for your promotion as well. If you consistently apply these principles to your life, I'm convinced they will prepare you to face and maximize your most daunting God-given opportunities with courage, boldness and assurance! As a result, you will experience the joy that emanates from a prepared life. So, let me ask you, "Are you prepared for promotion?"

Do you know:

- Your **PURPOSE**? *(Answers the question: WHY?)*
  - Have you discovered your purpose?
  - Why are you here? Why has God given you life?

- Your **PLAN?** *(Answers the question: HOW?)*
  - Do you have a strategy for your life?
  - What are the specific steps involved in your plan?

- Your **PERIOD** *(Answers the question: WHEN?)*
  - Are you able to discern your set time and season(s)?
  - Do you know when to move forward? or stand still?

- Your **PEOPLE?** *(Answers the question: WHO?)*
  - Who are the critical people that should support you?
  - Have you identified your team, friend(s), associates, enemies, mentors, mentees, etc.?

IT'S YOUR TURN NOW!

- Have you identified the different role(s) and function(s) others play in your life?

🔑 Your **PROFESSION** *(Answers the question: WHAT are you SAYING?)*

- Do you understand the creative power of your words?
- What are you professing about yourself?

🔑 Your **POSITION** *(Answers the question: WHERE is your INFLUENCE?)*

- What is your current position of influence?
- Where should you use your position of influence to help others?

🔑 Your **PRICE** *(Answers the question: HOW MUCH? How MUCH will it COST?)*

- What value will you place on your assignment(s) and purpose?
- How much are you willing to pay to know and fulfill your assignment(s) and purpose?

🔑 Your **PROMOTION** *(Answers the question of: REWARD?)*

- What are the results/benefits of a principle-driven life?
- Who benefits from your advancement?

Unlocked Doors of Opportunities

Preparation unlocks doors of opportunities that put you in a position for promotion. Promotion is not only about benefits, rewards, and what's in it for me. But God also desires to promote you to positions of power so that you can be a blessing to someone else. Are you in a position to help someone else? Or is it all about you?

If you are unable to say yes, then it's your turn to get prepared. Section IV will challenge you to do the work required to prepare yourself for future opportunities and promotions that's waiting on you. Prepare, prepare, prepare!

CHAPTER 7

My Purpose

Answers the question: WHY?

"A Woman who walks in Purpose doesn't have to chase people or Opportunities. Her Light Causes People and Opportunities to pursue her." – unknown

"For if you remain silent at this time, liberation and rescue will arise for the Jews from another place, and you and your father's house will perish [since you did not help when you had the chance]. And who knows whether you have attained royalty for such a time as this [and for this very purpose]?" (Esther 4:14 Amp)

Do You Know Your Purpose?

The first principle to understand and incorporate in your life if you're going to be prepared for your turn is purpose. Purpose answers the question "WHY?" Purpose is the reason for the existence of a person or thing and gives meaning to life. Purpose is the "why" of life. There comes a time in all of our lives when we need to stop and answer the question, "Why am I here?" Do you know why God has allowed you the privilege of gracing

IT'S YOUR TURN NOW!

this planet with your presence? Do you know your purpose? God has reserved a unique purpose just for YOU. A purpose that's bigger than you. No one can fulfill it, but you. More importantly, you can't fulfill it if you don't know it. So, it's time to discover it.

I often quote the late Dr. Myles Monroe's famous saying, "Where purpose is not known, abuse is inevitable." He defined the word abuse as abnormal use. When a person doesn't know the purpose for another person or thing, the only thing he can do is to abnormally use it. Abuse describes the actions of any person who abnormally uses another individual or thing. For example, child-abuse, wife-abuse, and drug abuse to name a few.

Did you know you can abnormally use yourself? When you don't know why you have been given life, all you can do is abuse it. You have been created by God to fulfill a specific purpose. God told Jeremiah, *"Before I shaped you in the womb, I knew all about you. Before you saw the light of day, I had holy plans for you: A prophet to the nations—that's what I had in mind for you"* Jeremiah 1:5 (NLT). Just like God had a specific plan in mind for Jeremiah before he ever showed up on planet earth, he has a plan in mind for you too. He is committed to bringing His plans and purposes to pass in your life. Proverbs 19:21 (AMP) says, *Many plans are in a man's mind, but it is the Lord's purpose for him that will stand (be carried out)."* If God is committed to your purpose, shouldn't you be committed to it as well?

Finding Purpose

I'm going to ask you again, "Do you know God's purpose for your life?" I'm not asking you about *your* purpose, but rather the purpose God had in mind for you before you were conceived in your mother's womb. If you don't know God's purpose for your life, I'm sure you're asking, "How do I find out my God-ordained purpose?" You start by asking the one who created you and gave you life. Since, God is your creator, ask Him. Matthew 7:7-8 (KJV) says, *"Ask, and it shall be given you; seek, and ye shall find; knock, and it shall be opened unto you: For every one that asketh receiveth; and he that seeketh findeth; and to him that knocketh it shall be opened."* This is no cavalier attitude when it comes to this kind of asking. This is a persistent search that increases in intensity every time you petition the one who has the answer. In this case that person is God. Finding your purpose is a process of discovery that God reveals only to the avid seeker.

> Finding your purpose is a process of discovery that God reveals only to the avid seeker.

A great way to find your unique purpose is to start with the universal purpose for all of mankind. The Apostle Paul defines "why" God ultimately created all of mankind. He tells us, *"we are God's masterpiece who has been created anew in Christ Jesus"*, for the expressed purpose of doing the *"good works he planned for us long ago"* Ephesians 2:10 (NLT). A key step in finding out why you are here, is by doing good works. Find something good

IT'S YOUR TURN NOW!

to do and do it with all of your heart and with all your might unto God! 1 Corinthians 10:31 (KJV) says, *"Whether therefore ye eat, or drink, or whatsoever ye do, do all to the glory of God."*

Purpose vs. Assignment

There is a difference between purpose and assignment. Your purpose never changes but your assignment does. Remember, purpose answers the question why. When you know your "why" you can define your "what". The problem many people have is they know their "what" and have no clue about their "why". They're more concerned about "what" to do and haven't first identified "why" they should do it. Anytime you do your "what" before you know your "why", you're out of order and anything out of order can't be used.

> Anytime you do your "what" before you know your "why", you're out of order and anything out of order can't be used.

Have you ever walked up to a vending machine expecting to get a snack and there was a sign on it that read, "OUT OF ORDER"? What was your response? More than likely, you just walked away because you realized it couldn't be used. Perhaps that may be the reason so many opportunities are walking away from you. You have no idea "why" you are doing "what" you are doing, and consequently, you're out of order and God can't use you.

Please don't get discouraged if you have asked God to show you His purpose for your life and you're still not certain. I want to be candid and say, I didn't know or understand my purpose immediately either. I came to know and understand my purpose through many years of intentionally seeking the face of God for it. It was a process of discovery: I searched Scripture with the expectation that the Holy Spirit would reveal God's purpose for my life through His Word; I read books and listened to inspiring qualified teachers and speakers who knew their purpose and was willing to share their process of discovery; I fasted and prayed to develop a sensitivity to discern the will of God for my life; and as I remained diligent to seek Him, He continued to reveal my purpose piece by piece. It's much like putting a puzzle together. It slowly began to take shape as I continued my search believing God would reward me for my diligence according to Hebrews 11:6 (KJV). *"But without faith it is impossible to please him: for he that cometh to God must believe that he is, and that he is a rewarder of them that diligently seek him."* And still today, the details of the entire puzzle isn't complete. God continues to unfold the details of His plan and purpose for my life as I develop my faith through His Word. If your purpose is going to be revealed to you, it will require your dedicated focused attention.

Esther's Assignments and Purpose

As a result of Mordecai's relentless pursuit of Esther's assistance in saving the Jewish nation, Esther came to know the

IT'S YOUR TURN NOW!

difference between her purpose and her assignment. Throughout her story we see the various assignments she accepted along her destiny track towards fulfilling her destined purpose.

Her first assignment and door of opportunity was extended to her by her surrogate father, Mordecai. Her assignment was to represent her nation in a one hundred and twenty-seven provinces beauty contest that stretched from India to Ethiopia, in search of the next queen of the Persian Empire. Her second assignment came in the form of a request from Mordecai to speak to the king to spare the lives of the Jewish nation, an assignment that could have very well cost Esther her life. Reluctantly, she accepted the assignment and that assignment revealed her purpose and positioned her to change the fate of the entire Jewish nation.

I know Esther started out a little reluctant to step up and take her turn, but by the time she stood up to speak, she was fully persuaded and prepared. She courageously spoke on behalf of a people who couldn't speak for themselves. Queen Esther answered, *"If I have found favor in your eyes, O King, and if it please the king, give me my life, and give my people their lives. "We've been sold, I and my people, to be destroyed—sold to be massacred, eliminated. If we had just been sold off into slavery, I wouldn't even have brought it up; our troubles wouldn't have been worth bothering the king over"* (Esther 7:3-4). Can you feel her passion?

ALMA GORDON BAMBERG

Purpose Found in Passion

Your purpose can be found in what you are passionate about. Passion is a powerful indicator of purpose. What are you passionate about? What do you have a strong desire to do, have or become? What is that "thing" that causes you to express an intense interest or enthusiasm for? Let me be clear, passion is more than a strong emotion. Emotions can quickly fade, but passion, even when it seems as if you have none, somewhere in the recesses of your heart, passion is there waiting to be ignited. Passion comes from a deeper place than emotions. Passion is the fuel that keeps you going, even when you feel you can't go any further. Passion is that desire you can't get away from. That desire is in your dreams when you sleep. You wake up with it. It's in your thoughts throughout the day. Passion exposes the purpose for which you were born and refuses to leave you alone until it drives you to its destined end. *"If you can't figure out your purpose, figure out your passion. For your passion will lead you right into your purpose."* – TD Jakes

> "If you can't figure out your purpose, figure out your passion. For your passion will lead you right into your purpose."
> – TD Jakes

The passion that exposes purpose has eternal value. It drives you to do something that is bigger than yourself. It adds value to others that will continue after you are dead and gone. It's a passion to make a difference in the lives of others. Do you have a passion to make a difference? If so, it could be an indicator of your purpose.

Purpose Found in Your Strengths

Your purpose can be found in your strengths. What are your God-given gifts, talents, and abilities? Romans 12:6a (NLT) says, God, in his grace, *"has given us different gifts for doing certain things well."* What do you do well?

The Bible is very clear about the gifts God gives. There are "gift "chapters in the New Testament. The *Gifts of the Spirit* or the Spiritual Gifts are found in I Corinthians 12:8-12; the *Purpose for Spiritual Gifts* is found in I Corinthians 14:3; the *Five-fold Ministry Gifts* are found in Ephesians 4:11-13; and the seven *Foundational Gifts* in the body of Christ are found in Romans 12:4-8.

The *Gifts of the Spirit* falls into three categories. I like to call them Spoken Gifts, Power Gifts and Revelation Gifts:

1) The *Spoken Gifts* minister to us spiritually.
    - divers tongues;
    - interpretation of tongues, and
    - prophecy

2) The *Power Gifts* minister to us physically.
    - working of miracles,
    - gift of faith, and

- gift of healing

3) The *Revelation Gifts* minister to us emotionally.
    - word of knowledge,
    - word of wisdom, and
    - discerning of spirits

The *Five-fold Ministry Gifts* are given to people who are called into the ministry usually on a full-time basis to edify and equip the saints. They are the *Apostle, Prophet, Evangelist, Pastor* and *Teacher*. These gifts are given to help the Believer mature in their Christian walks.

Each born-again believer is given a *Foundational Gift*. These seven gifts – *prophecy, serving, teaching, exhortation, giving, organization, and mercy* – show us our position and the position of others within the Body of Christ. One of the best ways to retain your passion *(excitement, and enthusiasm)* is to determine and operate within your place in the Body of Christ. Many times, we try to operate in an area of ministry to which we have not been called. To be effective, we must know where we fit. When we observe the seven gifts in operation throughout the Body of Christ, we see the complete ministry of Jesus Christ and we clearly understand how much we need the rest of the body. Sometimes we want to be the Lone Ranger. But we all need each other; and, without every gift operating, we will miss the completeness of Christ.

> "What comes easy to you but harder to other people?... What would you do for years and never get paid for it? ... How can you be of service?"
> - Farrah Gray

Finally, what are your *natural gifts*? What are those

things you do well that you've not been trained to do? What comes second nature to you? What is it that you do well with little or no effort? What are your natural bents? Is it cooking, dancing, writing, talking, or making others laugh? Don't discount the smallest detail. Your natural gifts are directional signs pointing you to your purpose and destiny. Farrah Gray, an American businessman, investor, author, columnist, and motivational speaker who began his entrepreneurial career at the age of six selling homemade lotion and hand-painted rocks door-to-door said: *"If you want to find what God put you here to do, ask yourself three questions. First question: What comes easy to you but harder to other people? The second question is: What would you do for years and never have to get paid for it? Third, ask yourself: How can you be of service?"*

Purpose Found in Another Person's Purpose

I hear it said all the time, "I don't know what my purpose is". Could it be that your purpose is found within a greater purpose? Every great purpose requires people to bring it to pass: The disciples found their purpose in Jesus' purpose; Jonathan found his purpose in David's purpose; and the church in the book of Acts found their purpose in Paul's purpose. Let's take a closer look at those who accompanied Paul on his missionary journey in Acts chapter 16. *"And a vision appeared to Paul in the night; There stood a man of Macedonia, and prayed him, saying, Come over into Macedonia, and help us. And after he had seen the vision, immediately **we** endeavored to go into Macedonia, assuredly gathering that the Lord had called **us** for to preach the gospel unto them."* (Acts 16:9-10 KJV)

> Where there are no people the vision perishes.

It's interesting to note the pronouns "we" and "us" in those verses. Paul was the one who saw the vision, but the vision was so big, it required more than Paul to accomplish it. Verse ten said Paul's companions got busy immediately making their way to Macedonia. They had no doubt that the call of the Lord was not just to Paul but to them as well. The call was bigger than Paul, it required their assistance. Proverbs 29:18a says, *"Where there is no vision, the people perish...".* And that is true. But let's look at the flip side of that verse. Where there are no people the vision perishes.

My Purpose and Assignments

Let me use myself as an example to explain the difference between my purpose and my assignments. My purpose is to *bring order out of chaos* and is primarily seen as a *developer of human potential.* I was born to *encourage, empower, equip. evangelize and enjoy life to the fullest.* This is why I exist. I help others develop and maximize their God-given potential. A major characteristic of as a developer of human potential is to 1) give hope by helping others realize what is possible for them; and 2) to show them how to bring that potential to pass in their lives. Bringing order requires strategic planning and if anyone knows me, I am a planner. I am an organizer. I'm naturally inclined to coordinate, arrange and manage people, things and situations. My automatic response to any task or situation is to think: What is the strategy? What are the steps? What is the plan of action to accomplish the goal? This dominate trait is evident in "what I do".

"What I do", are my assignments and are subject to change. Consequently, I will have more than one assignment in my lifetime and can have multiple assignments at the same time. My assignments are altered by the times and seasons of my life and

IT'S YOUR TURN NOW!

will vary in degrees of importance. Again, my assignment is my "what" and is subject to change. So, the question is: How is my purpose seen in my assignments? Here are a few examples of assignments I've had over the course of my life: wedding coordinator, floral designer, fashion designer and seamstress, interior decorator, choir director, praise and worship leader, computer programmer, database administrator(IBM), church administrator, systems analyst, speaker, school teacher, preacher, evangelist and executive pastor. What is the common thread throughout all of these assignments? The common thread is the ability to communicate structure and order. The Oxford Dictionary defines order as the arrangement or disposition of people or things in relation to each other according to a particular sequence, pattern, or method.

I have an innate ability to bring order to people, things, situations and systems. That is the way my creator has designed me to function and I function in accordance with my purpose. This explains why I'm more apt to see things that are out of order. Why? Because I'm wired to put it in order. This also explains why I have been given such a keen attention to details. I notice details that others never see. I can't get upset because they didn't see what I see. They're just not wired that way. Everything about us is the way it is to facilitate our God-given assignments and purpose.

> Everything about us is the way it is to facilitate our God-given purpose.

Joyce Meyers says it this way, "Your *who* is different from your *do*". In other words, you might do this and you might do that, but that's not who you are. We often define ourselves by the assignments, roles and functions we're asked to perform. For example, I am a wife but that is not who I am, that's a role and a function I have chosen to accept and carry out. If being a wife was my "who", God forbid if I were to get a divorce. Who will I be if I'm no longer married? This is why being a wife cannot be a woman's purpose and reason for existence. Being a wife is an assignment a woman chooses to accept. And might I add, it is a mission. Do you remember the recurring quote from the television series *Mission Impossible: "should you choose to accept this mission..."?* I must say, with God, the mission of marriage is possible. I hope this gives you a clearer picture of the difference between your assignment and your purpose.

IT'S YOUR TURN NOW!

IT'S YOUR TURN NOW TO WORK ON YOU

Self-Reflection Exercise:

Ask yourself –

1. I believe my God-given purpose Is _____
   _____
   _____

2. I am passionate about _____
   _____
   _____

3. What do I have a strong desire to do, have or become?
   _____
   _____

4. What are my natural God-given gifts, talents, and abilities? What are my strengths? What do I do well? What is the common thread? _____
   _____
   _____

5. What is it that others constantly ask me: "How is it that you can do that?" _____
   _____
   _____

6. In what areas am I abnormally using or abusing my life?
   _____
   _____

CHAPTER 8

My Plan

Answers the question: HOW?

"Then Esther told them to reply to Mordecai, "Go, gather all the Jews that are present in Susa, and observe a fast for me; do not eat or drink for three days, night or day. I and my maids also will fast in the same way...". (Esther 4:15-16a Amp)

A plan answers the question, "How?" Now that you know your purpose, how will you fulfill it? How are you going to bring God's desires for you to pass? How are you going to accomplish your dreams and aspirations? If you know your purpose but don't have a plan, you won't know "how" to accomplish your purpose. A plan is a systematic approach to achieving a desired goal that's been worked out in advance. A plan is a strategy for fulfilling your God-given purpose. To be effective in any endeavor, you need a strategic plan.

IT'S YOUR TURN NOW!

A Wise Woman

By the third day of the fast, God had given Esther a carefully devised plan of action to redeem the Jewish nation from destruction. The bible says, *"Now it happened on the third day that Esther put on her royal robes and stood in the inner court of the king's palace, across from the king's house, while the king sat on his royal throne in the royal house, facing the entrance of the house. So, it was, when the king saw Queen Esther standing in the court, that she found favor in his sight, and the king held out to Esther the golden scepter that was in his hand. Then Esther went near and touched the top of the scepter."* (Esther 5:1-2 NKJV) Do you think it was coincidental that the king was in the perfect spot to see Esther in the inner court? No. When God gives you a plan, there's nothing coincidental about it. God will orchestrate the minutest details of your life to get you to where you need to be so that those of influence can extend favor to you. The Bible is clear. The Lord holds the heart of influential people in his hand and is able to channel it in whatever direction He desires it to go. (Proverb 21:1 NLT)

When the king asked Esther for her request, she didn't speak hastily. She was a wise woman who understood the art of building a proper foundation upon which her request could securely rest. She refused to destroy her God-given opportunity with an unruly tongue. The book of wisdom says a wise woman knows how to properly build ..., *but a foolish woman destroys* what she builds *by what she does* Proverb 14:1 (NCV). What are you saying or doing that is destroying what you've built? Esther was careful to do everything in accordance with the plan she had received during her time of fasting. She carefully observed all that God had instructed her to do. She wasn't hasty with her request. She worked her plan and the plan worked for her.

Her request began with what might appear to be insignificant and contrary to what she was offered by the king. You see, the king was willing to give Esther whatever she wanted up to half of the kingdom. You wouldn't think inviting her enemy to dinner would be top on her agenda nor would it be the path to her enemy's demise. But God has a way of making your enemies your footstool. His ways are beyond what you could ever imagine. His thoughts are not your thoughts. The prophet Isaiah reminds us of that in Isaiah 55:8(KJV). God's *"...thoughts are not your thoughts, neither are his ways your ways..."*

Tailor-Made Plan

I'm sure we've all been asked, "What do you want to be when you grow up?" or "What do you want to do when you grow up?" As young kids and even as adults, it's often difficult to answer that question. But inevitably, we did our best to answer it even if we didn't know the answer. Perhaps as you grew older, you were heavily influence by your peers and loved ones who led you in a direction that had no correlation to the plans and purposes God had in mind when He created you. Just maybe you followed

IT'S YOUR TURN NOW!

the direction of well-meaning others not knowing that God was the one who had the correct answer all the time.

The book of Proverbs gives insight into God's perspective when it comes to the plans we make for ourselves. *"We can make our own plans, but the Lord gives the right answer. People may be pure in their own eyes, but the Lord examines their motives. Commit your actions to the Lord, and your plans will succeed. The Lord has made everything for his own purposes, even the wicked for a day of disaster... We can make our plans, but the Lord determines our steps."* (Proverbs 16:1-4, 9 NLT) If you've made plans for your life that aren't working, ask yourself, "Have I committed my actions to the Lord?" Then, ask God to order your steps. It's only when you submit and commit what you do to God, will your plans succeed.

> "Commit your actions to the Lord, and your plans will succeed."

God has a plan perfectly suited for the purpose He has for you. Your purpose is specific to you, much like a tailored-made outfit. Whenever an outfit has been tailor-made, it's been made to perfectly fit the individual using their specific measurements. And just like that tailored-made outfit, God has a tailored-made plan that's specific and perfect for your purpose too! No one can do what you have been created to do the way you do it. You cannot be duplicated. Imitated? Yes. Duplicated? No. You are an original.

What Makes a Plan Successful?

Genesis, the book of beginnings, shares a story with us about a people who had a selfish plan to build a city and tower that would make a name for themselves. Then they said, *"Come, let's build a great city for ourselves with a tower that reaches into the sky. This will make us famous and keep us from being scattered all over the world"* Genesis 11:4 (NLT). God wasn't pleased with their motivation and reasoning for wanting to build this city so He halted their plans by confusing their language. However, it is important to note the power in having a workable plan:

1) <u>Their plan attracted the attention of God.</u>
   "Then the Lord came down to see the city and the tower that the humans built." Genesis 11:5 CEB;

2) <u>God said their plan would have succeeded if He had not stopped them.</u>
   "And the Lord said... all they plan to do will be possible for them" Genesis 11:6 CEB.

Let's take a look at God's assessment of why their wicked plan would be successful. The amplified Bible says, *"Behold, they are one [unified] people, and they all have the same language."* And as a result, *"This is only the beginning of what they will do [in rebellion against Me], and now no evil thing they imagine they can do*

> ...success hinges on being unified...speaking the same language and having the ability to imagine possibilities...

will be impossible for them" Genesis 11:6. WOW! Their success hinged on being a *unified people*, speaking the *same language* and having the *ability to imagine the possibilities* of what they could do. What an incredible combination! If you want your plans to succeed, it would be wise to consider these factors as well. How unified are the people involved in your plan(s)? Or better yet, let me ask: Are you in agreement with your own plan(s) or are you vacillating from day to day? What are you and those around you saying about your plan(s)? What are you and those involved with your plan(s) envisioning on the canvas of your imaginations about the possibilities of what could be accomplished?

Developing My Plan

At this point I'm sure you're wondering if I could help you know where to begin as you contend with the thought of developing and building your own personal plan. And the answer is, yes, I will help you.   I think a great place to start is in Luke Chapter 14. It provides sound instructions when considering building anything, whether it is a life, career, building, family, business or relationship, etc.   Let me warn you up front, this passage of scripture can be somewhat intimidating to those who have some unfinished business. But let me also encourage you not to allow the enemy to use this word to condemn you but rather convict you. Take comfort in Romans Chapter 8: *"Therefore there is now no condemnation [no guilty verdict, no punishment] for those who are in Christ Jesus [who believe in Him as personal Lord and Savior]"* (Romans 8:1 AMP).

In Chapter 14 of Luke, Jesus turns to a crowd of people who were following Him and began to admonish them as to what it would cost to be one of His disciples. Following Christ was no small matter. Jesus was straight up with those considering building a life as one of His disciples. He told them, they must be prepared to leave father and mother, wife, children, brothers and sisters, and even give up their own lives, otherwise, they couldn't be His disciples. He further explained the endurance of their individual crosses they each must bear. So, as you develop your plan, I encourage you to seriously consider the following from Luke 14:28-34 (MSG).

*"Is there anyone here who, **planning to build** a new house, doesn't first sit down and figure the cost so you'll know if you can complete it? If you only get the foundation laid and then run out of money, you're going to look pretty foolish. Everyone passing by will poke fun at you: 'He started something he couldn't finish. Or can you imagine a king going into battle against another king without first deciding whether it is possible with his ten thousand troops to face the twenty thousand troops of the other? And if he decides he can't, won't he send an emissary and work out a truce? Simply put, if you're not willing to take what is dearest to you, whether plans or people, and kiss it good-bye, you can't be my disciple. "Salt*

IT'S YOUR TURN NOW!

is excellent. But if the salt goes flat, it's useless, good for nothing. "Are you listening to this? Really listening?"

Careful Analysis Required

The first point Jesus makes to the crowd was to sit down! In other words, I want you to stop and assume a position of rest. In the day and age in which we live, taking time to stop is often a difficult task. Even when most of us are reclining in a position of rest our minds find it difficult to do the same. Jesus emphasizes the importance of stopping before commencing to build. Devising a plan is a serious decision-making process that requires a rested mental state of being.

Secondly, Jesus points out the importance of counting the cost of making the decision to follow Him. Counting the cost requires analyzing your current state. It requires: First of all, careful assessment of everything needed to accomplish the task; and secondly, estimation of what you currently have and what you will need to acquire to accomplish the task at hand. Counting the cost involves devising a plan. Every plan should consist of the steps needed to move you from where you are to where you would like to be. From this passage of Scripture, we can surmise seven questions to ponder when establishing a plan for any facet of your life.

1) <u>Have you established the desired goal/end result BEFORE starting?</u>

Where are you going? Don't be so anxious to start without first defining the destination. God is a perfect example of this type of planning in Isaiah 46:10 (KJV). The way God starts his planning process is by *"Declaring the end from the beginning..."*. The Expanded Bible says it like this: *"...From the beginning I told you what would happen in the end. A long time ago [From ancient times] I told you things that have not yet happened. When I plan something, it happens [...saying, "My counsel will stand"]. What I want to do, I will do"* (Isaiah 46:9-10 EXB).

2) <u>Do you know what is needed to reach the desired goal/end result?</u>
   Have you determined what human, physical, and financial resources are needed to finish what you plan to build?

3) <u>Do you know how much is needed to reach the desired goal/end result?</u>
   Do you have enough resources *(human, physical, financial, etc.)* for the entire plan?

4) <u>Are you prepared for the emotional FIGHT?</u>
   Have you considered the emotional impact of not finishing what you started? Have you considered the emotional impact of success? Have you considered warranted and unwarranted criticism(s)?

IT'S YOUR TURN NOW!

5) <u>Have you built your FAITH muscles to endure a spiritual FAITH fight of this magnitude?</u>

    Every faith fight is not the same and doesn't require the same level of strength. To win your faith fight, your faith muscles must match the faith fight you're in. Have you assessed the strength of the spiritual resources you have? Are they comparable to what is needed in the natural? Are your natural and spiritual resources in the same weight class. In other words, do you have a realistic understanding of what you have in the natural and what you will need to "faith-In" spiritually to get the job done?

6) <u>Do you have a Plan B prepared just in case your Plan A doesn't work?</u>

    If you see where you cannot accomplish your plan the way you originally planned, do you have a Plan B waiting in the wings? Before God created Adam and gave him Plan A, commanding him not to eat of the tree of good and evil, He had a Plan B just in case Adam chose to disobey. Jesus Christ was God's Plan B, waiting in the wings to die for mankind just in case Plan A failed. Revelation 13:8 (KJV) says, Jesus was *"the Lamb slain from the foundation of the world."* So, before God ever carried out His plan to create Adam, Jesus had already decided to die a substitutionary death.

7) <u>Have you identified at what point you should go with your Plan B?</u>

Don't mistake faith for pride or shame and wait until it's too late to rebound and enforce your Plan B. Be honest with God and yourself to know when it's time to let go and move on.

TAKE ACTION

A plan means absolutely nothing if you don't take action. Thinking about the questions to establish a plan of action is not enough. You've got to get those thoughts out of your head and on paper. Write it down! Write down what are you envisioning. Write the vision God has shown you in your imagination. A plan is accelerated once it's written down. And a plan is not clear until it's written. The prophet Habakkuk bears witness to this in chapter 2:2: *"... Write the vision, and make it plain upon tables, that he may run that readeth it."*

A plan is a documented approach of achieving the specified vision, goal, or idea that has been locked up in your mind. When you document your plan, you're providing yourself with a way to get out, what you've envisioned inside. A written plan is the doorway to unlock your mind. My sister, it's within your power to

> A plan is accelerated once it's written down.

IT'S YOUR TURN NOW!

free yourself! Don't allow fear to paralyze you. It's your move. What are you going to do Now?

IT'S YOUR TURN NOW TO WORK ON YOU

Self-Reflection Exercise:

Ask yourself –

1) My final outcome/destination/goal is_____
   _____
   _____
   _____

2) What are the resources (human, physical, financial, etc.) required to carry out my plan?_____
   _____
   _____
   _____

3) How can I build my faith muscles to endure the spiritual faith fight involved in working my plan?___
   _____
   _____
   _____

4) What is my "Plan B" just in case my "Plan A" doesn't work out? Is my plan written down? If not, why haven't I written it down? *(I need to make sure my plan is written down.)*_____
   _____
   _____

IT'S YOUR TURN NOW!

CHAPTER 9

My Period

Answers the question: WHEN?

"There is a season (a time appointed) for everything and a time for every delight and event or purpose under heaven"
—Ecclesiastes 3:1 (AMP)

The period has to do with timing! Timing is everything. Timing answers the question of "when". I'm sure you would agree with me that having a baby is a good thing at the right time. But having a baby at the wrong time can cause major problems. You've got to ask yourself, when is it the right time to do this or to do that?

How Long is it Going to Take?

It wasn't until the *seventh year* of the king's reign that Esther's turn came to go before the king. Let's do the math. Esther entered the palace in the third year and didn't come before the king until the seventh year. Seven years minus three years equals four years. Four years, young virgins were going in and out of the king's quarters with dashed dreams of being the next queen of the Persian

IT'S YOUR TURN NOW!

Empire. For four long years Esther patiently waited her turn. For four long years she said to herself, "I know my turn is coming."

When Esther's turn finally came, *"The king loved Esther more than all the other women, and she obtained grace and favor in his sight more than all the virgins; so. he set the royal crown upon her head and made her queen instead of Vashti"* Esther 2:17 (NKJV). I can imagine the king saying, "Esther is the one! Let's make Esther the new Persian Queen. We can stop all these one-night stands. I've had four years of nights, I'm pretty tired" (In the voice of Forest Gump). Just imagine, four years of turns with young virgin women.

In the meantime, a law had been enforced throughout the land from India to Ethiopia that all the Jews would be destroyed (Esther 8:9). The Bible says it was in the *twelfth year* of the king, that Haman, the enemy of the Jews deceived the king into signing a decree that would destroy the entire Jewish Nation.

Now, let's recap the timeline. Esther entered the royal contest in the *third year* of the king's reign. In the seventh year she's shown favor by the king and crowned queen. Then, in the twelfth year she puts her life on the line and petitions the king on behalf of her people. That meant four years had passed since she initially entered the palace and was crowned queen, then five more years passed and she's faced with the dilemma of revealing her nationality and saving her people. It was a total of nine long years. That's right, nine years of patiently waiting her turn.

ALMA GORDON BAMBERG

Growth and Development

Because Biblical numerology has always fascinated me, I decided to research the meaning of the number nine. I was amazed at how much it coincided with what was transpiring during this time of Esther's life.

Nine has to do with finality or judgement, generally, at the time of judging a person and his works. Also, the number nine is used to define the perfect movement of God. It is the number of those who accomplish His divine will. Biblical number nine stands for a complete cycle of growth and is the number of patience. [3]

Now isn't that something? After nine years of waiting, God was ready to move on behalf of His people. He had been preparing an orphan Jewish girl to one day rise up and deliver an entire nation for extinction. Esther's nine-year preparation period allowed her time to develop and grow into the courageous deliverer she was meant to be. Her turn had come. It reminds me of the nine months in which an embryo grows and develops into a healthy fetus preparing for delivery.

The perfect time had finally arrived for Haman, the enemy of the Jews, to be judged for his wicked works against Mordecai and the people of God. And Esther had been chosen by God to be the instrument He would use to bring about this judgement. She patiently waited for the perfect timing of God to accomplish His divine will. Esther had to wait until her turn without full understanding. She had to wait without knowing the real reason for which she had been brought to the palace. And now, her turn had come. Esther's God-given purpose was at hand. She was confronted with a chance to use her position of power and influence to make a difference in the longevity of an entire nation. Each time, Esther was presented with a choice to accept her turn, she chose to take it! And this time was no different. WHY? Because she used her wait time wisely. She was prepared!

Patiently Waiting

Waiting is not based on age, gender, race or class. We all have to wait our turn. The question is how will we wait? The Psalmist tells us how to wait. He said, *"I waited patiently for the Lord; and he inclined unto me, and heard my cry. Rest in the Lord, and wait patiently for him..."* (Ps. 40:1a; 37:7a KJV). Patience is a key component of the faith process that undergirds, strengthens and supports your faith until the manifestation comes. *The Greek translation of the word patience is hupomone (hoop-om-on-ay') which means cheerful, hopeful, continuance while in the waiting process.* [4] Please hear me, just because God gave you an idea, a Word, or a promise doesn't mean you're to move on it immediately. Preparation is required. Preparation requires waiting and waiting requires patience. Remember, Ecclesiastes chapter three: There is "a time appointed for everything."

Throughout the preparation process your faith will be tested, but don't worry, that's the time for patience to go to work on your behalf. The book of James 1:3-4 (KJV) is clear about that: *"the trying of your faith worketh patience. But let patience have her perfect work, that ye may be perfect and entire, wanting nothing."* I love the Amplified Bible rendering of verse three, it says: *"Be assured that the testing of your faith [through experience] produces endurance(patience) [leading to spiritual maturity, and inner peace]. And let endurance (patience) have its perfect result and do a thorough work, so that you may be perfect and completely developed [in your faith], lacking in nothing."*

Patience goes to work after you release your faith for the promises of God. It props you up and braces you as you wait. Patience acts as a spiritual incubator controlling your environment, protecting you from contagious intolerance, and assisting you in the spiritual growth and development of your spirit man. Patience is necessary because you must respect the time factor. God loves you too much to present you with an opportunity that you've not been given adequate time to prepare for. God will wait until you are

> Patience acts as a spiritual incubator controlling your environment, protecting you from contagious intolerance and assisting you in the spiritual growth and development of your spirit man.

IT'S YOUR TURN NOW!

spiritually mature enough to handle your turn. So, don't despise the wait time, prepare yourself, NOW!

No Time to Waste

Understanding the timing of God is critical. There is a designated time for you to fulfill God's plan for your life. It's time now to get ready! You don't have time to waste. There are many things you can afford to waste but time is not one of them. I don't advise it, but you can waste your money and if you live long enough and work hard enough, there is a great possibility that you can make more money. But time wasted can never be recovered. This moment, when it passes, you can never get it back. So, manage your time wisely and please don't allow anyone, including yourself, to waste it.

Have you ever called a friend and when you asked that friend what they were doing and the response was, *"nothing"*? Giving you that response a few times is all right, but if that's the response every time you talk to that person, just maybe it's time to get a new friend. I'm just saying. Time is a very precious commodity and I want to remind you, you're on the clock. Tick Tock. Time is passing and you've got to get prepared before your next God-given opportunity arrives.

ALMA GORDON BAMBERG

Time vs. Turn

When I speak of time, it denotes a period of time, much like a season, for example summer time and winter time. It's a duration of time with a start date and an end date. Summer season has a specific start date and end date regardless of how the climate feels. Ecclesiastes is clear about time. To everything there is a season and a time to every purpose under heaven. We're told there is, *"A time to be born and a time to die; A time to plant and a time to harvest; A time to kill and a time to heal; A time to tear down and a time to build up; A time to cry and a time to laugh; A time to grieve and a time to dance; A time to scatter stones and a time to gather stones; A time to embrace and a time to turn away; A time to search and a time to quit searching; A time to keep and a time to throw away; A time to tear and a time to mend; A time to be quiet and a time to speak; A time to love and a time to hate; A time for war and a time for peace"* Eccl 3:2-8 (NLT). There's an opportune time for everything.

But when I speak of a TURN, it's different from TIME. A turn denotes a specific moment within a given time period much like a designated turn to bat in a baseball game. It's a set time. It reminds me of Psalms 102:13 KJV: *"Thou shalt arise, and have mercy upon Zion: for the time to favour her, yea, the set time, is come"*. God has designated a time that has been set for all of us! I've come to realize it could be your time and not your turn. Why is it important to make that

> ...it could be your time and not your turn.

distinction? Often, when God called someone in the Bible to perform a mighty feat, it didn't happen immediately.

David is a great example of someone who had to spend a great deal of time waiting for his turn. He was anointed by the Prophet Samuel to be king over Israel when he was but a shepherd boy, but it took approximately fifteen years before He was actually appointed king over Judah (2 Samuel 2:1-5) and another five or so years before becoming king over Israel (2 Samuel 5:1-5). While the historian Josephus says that he was ten years old when Samuel anointed him, modern commentaries place the age at around fifteen to twenty-five. What we are assured of based on 2 Samuel 5:4 is that David was thirty years old when he became king of Israel, and he reigned forty years. This meant David waited 5-20 years of his life to be appointed king of Israel. As a young lad, he was anointed, but not appointed! When Samuel anointed David king, it was his time, but it was not his turn.

God shows up in the life of Abram and tells him I am changing your name from Abram to Abraham. The reason God changes his name was because He was in the process of making Abram the Father of many nations. At that period in time Abram wasn't father of any, but God declared He would make him the father of many. It was a twenty-five-year process before what God called Him became a reality in his life. The moment God spoke the promise to Abraham was his *time*, but it was *NOT his turn.*

Gideon threshed wheat by the winepress, hiding from the Midianites "...*the angel of the Lord appeared unto him, and said,*

ALMA GORDON BAMBERG

The Lord is with thee, thou mighty man of valor" Judges 6:11-12 (KJV). At the moment the angel spoke, Gideon didn't look like a mighty man of valor nor was he behaving as a mighty man of valor. But by the time his turn rolled around to lead out in battle, he had built up the courage to do what God had chosen him to do. He took three hundred men and beat down the Midianites. It was his time, but it wasn't his turn.

Moses was indeed the man God raised up in the house of Pharaoh to deliver the children of Israel from Egyptian slavery. But before he could speak on God's behalf he had to spend forty years being educated in Egyptian wisdom and forty years tending Jethro's flock in obscurity. God earmarked Moses as a baby floating up the Nile River to confront the Pharaoh of Egypt to let God's people go! As a matter of fact, the moment Moses mother, Jochebed gave birth to him, it was his time, but it wasn't his turn. Finally, after 80 years of waiting, Moses' turn rolled around when he walked into Pharaoh's courts and commanded him to let God's people go!

Whenever God speaks, He speaks in present tense because He knows it's already done! And even though the thing that He spoke in your life hasn't come to pass in the natural, if you will prepare yourself now to walk in that promise, it's only a matter of time before it materializes, and what was spoken over your life then, will manifest now.

IT'S YOUR TURN NOW!

Can You Wait Your Turn?

Preparation is no cake walk, it's work and most of all, it requires time and patience! Esther was no exception; she had to endure the preparation process too and wait her turn! When we read the story of Esther it can be misconstrued that all of these events took place in a short period of time. For example, we might think:

- Immediately, the call was made for beautiful virgins to enter the royal contest to become the next queen of Persia;
- Then, Esther's cousin signed her up to be one of the contestants;
- She undergoes the twelve-month required beauty treatment;
- Without delay, she goes before the king and he selects her to be the next queen.
- Shortly thereafter, wicked Haman gets fed up with Mordecai's disrespect of not bowing down to him and so he has the king sign an edict to destroy all the Jews;
- Right away, Esther builds up enough courage to go before the king even if it costs her to lose her life;
- And instantly, she comes up with a plan to have the king reverse the law and like magic, the nation is saved.

Yes, that was the order of events, however, the events didn't take place in a short span of time. It's important to look at how much time transpired between those major events. Before I closely studied the life of Esther, I didn't realize how long it took for her to actually prepare to save her people. It wasn't until careful examination of the timeline that I understood the wait time.

The Bible says it was in the *third year* of the king's reign that Esther was brought into the Palace to enter the beauty contest after queen Vashti was removed from her royal position. For the next twelve months each young woman had to prepare herself to go before the king. Let me highlight the word "each". The New King James Version makes that point. *"Each young woman's turn came to go in to King Ahasuerus after she had completed twelve months' preparation, according to the regulations for the women, for thus were the days of their preparation apportioned: six months with oil of myrrh, and six months with perfumes and preparations for beautifying women. Thus prepared, each young woman went to the king..."* (Esther 2:12-13a NKJV) Can you imagine how many women there were waiting for their turn to spend just one night with the king with the hopes that she would find favor in his sight? Each woman was required to wait her turn and that included Esther.

IT'S YOUR TURN NOW!

Girl, You Got This

I, too, have found myself waiting for my turn. As I stated earlier, it was eight years ago when God spoke the words to me, "It's Your TURN!" But during the month of January of 2016, as I prepared for a women's conference, He said it again, only this time, the word "NOW" was added. At the end of the year, I was privileged to revisit the word I spoke in January as I watched a video of myself ministering it on my sister's iPad. *(Thank you, Cheryl, for that labor of love.)* As I watched myself, a fire was ignited in my soul. That day, I knew the time had come for me to step up and take my turn to share this word with my sisters all over the country and even the world. Eight years of waiting! Eight years of preparation to give birth to this word in this formate.

As I reflected on the word "now," it invoked a sense of urgency within me. I felt a sense of obligation to pen this book. So, in January of 2017, I got busy documenting my plan and establishing my timelines. I eagerly began writing and was amazed at the progress I was making. Two months into writing, the enemy began to throw all types of distractions my way and before long my drive and focus were totally gone. I found myself dead in the middle of James 1:1-8. My faith for this project was being tested, and I don't mean just one test, but one after another. They just kept coming. Even as I write today, I'm still in the midst of a major fight to complete this book, but I, like Esther refused to miss my turn! My emotions are under major attack, my relationships are under attack, my health is under attack, you name it, everything the enemy can throw my way is trying to stop me. But, I've come to realize I can't trust my emotions. In the words of Joyce Meyer, "your emotions are fickle". Your emotions are unpredictable. They are unstable and indecisive, so I made a choice to move forward on what I know to be true and stable, and that's God's Word to me.

> To my sister who feels a sense of urgency to step out and take your turn but fear, doubt and failure is daring you to move, do it anyway!

So, today, I want to say to my sister who feels a sense of urgency to step out and take your turn but fear, doubt and failure is daring you to move, do it anyway! Do it while you are afraid! Don't let anything or anyone stop you! Not distractions, not fear, not doubt, not your past mistakes, not the lack of money, nor the lack of education. Let NO-thing stop you! I'm going to tell you like one of my friends told me as I made a decision to step out and write this book: "Girl, you got this!" I close this chapter with a word from the Lord for you. If you fail to take your turn now, you're in jeopardy of missing your window of opportunity. It's a sobering fact, but for many of us, IT's NOW or NEVER!

IT'S YOUR TURN NOW!

IT'S YOUR TURN NOW TO WORK ON YOU

<u>Self-Reflection Exercise:</u>

Ask yourself –

1) What is the difference between my "time" and my "turn"? _____
   _____

2) What is it my "time" for? What is it my "turn" for?
   _____
   _____

3) What is my response when things don't happen immediately and I am required to wait? How does waiting affect me? _____
   _____

4) What is the difference between waiting and patiently waiting? _____
   _____

5) What's stopping me from taking my turn? *(Fear of failure? Distractions? Doubt? Past Mistakes? Lack of Money? Lack of Education? Etc.)* _____
   _____

CHAPTER 10

My People

Answers the Question: WHO?

"Success isn't something that happens overnight: it's a process. You have to nurture it along with continuous care, and the best way to do this is to have the right people working with you - not for you, but with you. I can dream alone and strive alone, but true success always requires the help and support of others." – Farrah Gray

"People" answers the question, who? Who should I allow in my life? Who are my friends? Who are my associates? Who are my enemies? Who am I to walk closely with and who am I to walk away from? Who are my mentors and who am I to mentor? It's important to know the people you're surrounded by. If you're going to be a prepared woman, you must carefully assess the people in your life. The people you associate with will either take you up or bring you down. It's your job to determine the people you will allow in your life and the role and function they will perform. People are essential to your progress and your proper

IT'S YOUR TURN NOW!

evaluation of each relationship will determine how far and how fast you will advance.

Proper Evaluation of Relationships

Developing a relationship with another person is not easy, but relationships are necessary. That's why it is important to evaluate your relationships and get a clear understanding of expectations and how those relationships are to function in your life. There were people throughout Esther's life that helped her and showed her favor giving her opportunity after opportunity to take her turn and fulfill her God-given assignments.

Who Are My Friends?

The term "friend" is held so loosely in our society today. Social media gives us permission to call everyone your friend. On Facebook you can accept people as your friend that you've never met. People walk up to me all the time and say, "Hi, I'm your friend on Facebook", and I don't even know their name. My criteria for friendship is quite different. Of course, I do realize there are different degrees of friendship but to be called my friend must begin with some knowledge of who you are and who I am. Bill Hybels, founding Pastor of Willow Creek Community Church, defined friendship like this: *"to know and be known"*.

A close friend is a true friend, a person you can truly be yourself around and feel absolutely comfortable with. There's no pretense or façade; you are free to be you, you're able to let it all hang out. I think a great way to describe a close friend is to think of them as a confidant. A person you can share your darkest secrets with and trust them not to share it with others. Do you have a close friend like that? Do you have a secret keeper for a friend? When I grew up, I heard the elderly call them bosom buddies. This is someone you can share the deepest issues of your heart with. There is a level of trust. You know this person loves you and has your back no matter what. There's a level of acceptance that supersedes perfection.

A close friend loves you even when you are wrong, and your faults are too numerous to count. By the same token, a true friend is not afraid to call you out when you are wrong. A true friend not only wants the best for you but will do everything within their power to help you succeed. If you've found that kind of friend, count yourself blessed and do everything you can to invest in that relationship.

The Bible informs us that true friendship starts with knowing how to be a friend first and goes beyond bloodline. It also helps us to understand that having too many so-called friends can bring devastation in your life. Proverbs 18:24 (AMP) says, *"The man of too many friends [chosen indiscriminately] will be broken in pieces and come to ruin, but there is a [true, loving] friend who [is reliable and] sticks closer than a*

> A true friend is willing to confront you and tell you the truth even if it hurts.

IT'S YOUR TURN NOW!

brother." Can you rely on the person(s) you call friend(s)?

Mordecai was a true friend to Esther. Yes, he was her cousin and adopted father, but I believe the reason He asked Esther to make such a difficult decision to put her life on the line, was because of their intimate relationship. He knew her. He took her in, not only into his home but in his heart. When Esther was a helpless orphan girl, *Mordecai* showed her favor and adopted her as his very own daughter. He had her back in her time of crisis, and he knew she would have his, in his time of crisis. That's true friendship. There was no way she would be able to live with herself knowing she had not done everything she could for the man who saved her life. Even in Esther's moments of doubt, Mordecai wasn't afraid to check her. A true friend doesn't only tell you what you want to hear. A true friend is willing to confront you and tell you the truth even if it hurts.

Who Are My Acquaintances?

Acquaintances are associates. Acquaintances are people you know to some extent, but you don't know them intimately. They are not a part of your inner circle of friends. Everyone who wants to be in your inner circle can't handle being that close to you. Please don't get me wrong. You need these connections, they are very important in your life. They include colleagues in business or work, carpool groups and workout partners, beauticians and bankers, and even within this group of acquaintances there are different levels or layers.

Esther needed Hegai. When she entered the twelve-month long beauty preparation period and the four years that followed as she waited to spend just one night with the king, she had *Hegai*, the one in charge of the harem. This connection was crucial in Esther's life and fulfillment of her purpose. She found favor in his sight as he extended preferential treatment by giving her the best room in the harem and the choicest attendants to assist her. God has already provided people to show you uncommon favor. Please know this, the favor is not about you alone. But it's about someone who cannot help themselves and God has placed you there to rescue them. The favor and everyone you need will be there when you need it. God knows the right connections you need. And just like Esther's connections, God has already placed them on your destiny track. As a matter of fact, they will be there waiting on you when you arrive. So, what are you waiting for? Keep moving.

Who Are My Enemies?

Haman was an enemy of the Jewish nation. And any enemy of the Jews was an enemy of Esther. He too, was a very critical part of Esther's life. There is no doubt what Haman did to the Jews was wrong, but Haman's devious scheme helped Esther. What he meant for evil worked out in her favor. His conniving plan became the catalyst that moved her closer to fulfilling the purpose for which she had been called. If he had never put out the edict to annihilate the Jews, the opportunity would never have presented

IT'S YOUR TURN NOW!

itself for her to speak on their behalf. As a matter of fact, the only reason Esther had been given the platform of the queen of Persia was to be the solution to the problem God knew Haman would devise.

And you, my sister, could it be that you're the solution to the problem you're in? Are you the answer to the problem you face? You don't have to fear. God has a way of making your enemies work for you, when they think they were working against you. The Bible says, God will make your enemy your footstool. In other words, you're going to be able to rest in the very thing that tried to cause you so much unrest.

There are people who did you wrong that I want you to know ultimately help you. I know it's difficult to see good coming out of a bad situation while you are going through it. But after all the dust has cleared, somehow, what happened to you, came to make you better, stronger or wiser. The person who did you wrong just might have been a tool in the hand of God preparing you for future opportunities. So, when you think about that person, instead of being upset, you might consider thanking God for them. When you look at how Judas betrayed Jesus, it was the betrayal that ushered Jesus into his purpose of redeeming mankind. You've got to learn how to keep going when people are for you and when people are against you.

> The person who did you wrong just might have been a tool in the hand of God preparing you for future opportunities.

ALMA GORDON BAMBERG

Positive and Negative Polarities

There's an unmatched power that's released when you allow both positive people and negative people to co-exist in your life. It reminds me of a battery. If you closely examine any battery you'll see both positive and negative polarities. You need both to produce power. You can't just have all positives and no negatives and expect to generate power. It'll never generate the power to produce anything. Maybe the reason you haven't produced what you desire to produce in your life is because you only surround yourself with people who are just like you. They think like you, act like you, enjoy the same foods, the same hobbies and they are only allowed to give you positive feedback. But you need a variety of people with different interest and cultural backgrounds in your life to make you a well-balanced productive individual.

Reproduction can only occur when two people of the opposite sex comes together. Two of the same sex cannot produce life. This process of reproduction is also seen in the life cycle of a plant. Reproduction doesn't occur without cross-pollination. Cross pollination occurs when pollen from the male reproductive organ of one plant is transferred to the female reproductive organ of

IT'S YOUR TURN NOW!

another plant by insects or wind. If the life cycle of plants requires other plants that are totally different from themselves to reproduce, what about you? You need people who are different from you to reproduce too. Why don't you take a moment to think about the people in your life? Do they think like you think? Dress like you dress? Do they all live in the same community that you live in or go to the same church that you attend? Do they always give you positive feedback or, are they free to share something that may rub you the wrong way? Now ask yourself: Who are the people that cause you to be productive? Who are the people that stimulate your creativity and growth? Comic actress, director, producer and writer, Amy Poehler, told a crowd of graduating seniors and their parents at Class Day, *"You can't do it alone...As you navigate through the rest of your life, be open to collaboration. Other people and other people's ideas are often better than your own. Find a group of people who challenge and inspire you, spend a lot of time with them, and it will change your life. No one is here today because they did it on their own... ."* Remember, powerful ideas are generated when we come together, so don't struggle alone.

Biblical Advice when Choosing the People in your Life

Does God have anything to say about the people in your life? He sure does! The Bible gives a lot of insight on this subject. Here are a few examples of what God has to say about relationships with others:

- *"The righteous choose their friends carefully, but the way of the wicked leads them astray."* Proverbs 12:26 (NIV)

- *"As iron sharpens iron, so a friend sharpens a friend."* Proverbs 27:17 (NLT)

- *"Walk with the wise and become wise; associate with fools and get in trouble."* Proverbs 13:20 (NLT)

- *"A friend is always loyal, and a brother is born to help in time of need."* Proverbs 17:17 (NLT)

- *"Two people are better than one because together they have a good reward for their hard work. If one falls, the other can help his friend get up. But how tragic it is for the one who is all alone when he falls. There is no one to help him get up."* Ecclesiastes 4:9-10 (GW)

- *"One who has unreliable friends soon comes to ruin, but there is a friend who sticks closer than a brother."* Proverbs 18:24 (NIV)

- *"Do not be misled: "Bad company corrupts good character."* 1 Corinthians 15:33 (NLT)

- *"A violent person entices their neighbor and leads them down a path that is not good."* Proverbs 16:29 (KJV)

IT'S YOUR TURN NOW!

- *"I did not sit with liars, and I will not be found among hypocrites. I have hated the mob of evildoers and will not sit with wicked people."* Psalm 26:4-5 (NOG - Names of God Bible)

- *"How blessed is the man who does not walk in the counsel of the wicked, Nor stand in the path of sinners, Nor sit in the seat of scoffers!"* Psalm 1:1 (NASB)

- *"Do not be a friend of one who has a bad temper, and never keep company with a hothead, or you will learn his ways and set a trap for yourself."* Proverbs 22:24-25 (GW)

- *"Now, what I meant was that you should not associate with people who call themselves brothers or sisters in the Christian faith but live in sexual sin, are greedy, worship false gods, use abusive language, get drunk, or are dishonest. Don't eat with such people."* 1 Corinthians 5:11(GW)

Words of Wisdom

- *"Associate yourself with people of good quality, for it is better to be alone then in bad company"* – Booker T. Washington

- *"If you allow people to make more withdrawals than deposits in your life, you will be out of balance and in the negative. Know when to close the account."* [5]

ALMA GORDON BAMBERG

- *"It's really important to have those people in your life who push you to be better, different." – Jesse Peyronel (Director & Writer)*

- *"Some people come into your life as blessings, others come into your life as lessons." – Mother Teresa*

IT'S YOUR TURN NOW TO WORK ON YOU

<u>Self-Reflection Exercise</u>:

Ask yourself –

1) Who are my:

    a. Friends? _____
   _____

    b. Acquaintances? _____
   _____

    c. Enemies? _____
   _____

    d. Mentor(s)? _____
   _____

    e. Mentee(s)? _____
   _____

2) What relationships do I need to redefine? _____
   _____
   _____
   _____

3) Who inspires me to be productive and stimulate my creativity and growth? _____
   _____
   _____
   _____

CHAPTER 11

---~ບໍ່ບ~---

My Profession

Answers the question: What are you SAYING?

When it came time for Esther to save her people, she spoke exactly what she desired. *"Esther said, "If it please the king, and if I have found favor with him, and if he thinks it is right, and if I am pleasing to him, let there be a decree that reverses the orders of Haman ...who ordered that Jews throughout all the king's provinces should be destroyed."* (Esther 8:5 NLT)

God had a covenant promise with the nation of Israel through Abraham to always preserve them. So, every time an enemy of the Jews rose up against them, God raised up a deliverer to save His people. And when Haman rose up against Mordecai and ultimately the entire Jewish nation, God raised up Esther. Once Esther realized she had been chosen to speak on behalf of her people, she held fast to her profession of faith and did not waver. As a result, God was faithful to fulfill His promise to preserve the Jewish nation.

Esther's beauty won her a beauty contest but it was what she said that triggered the fulfillment of the promise of God. This chapter explains how important profession is in bringing to pass the promises of God in the life of the Believer. The word profession and the word confession are both translated from the same Greek word and have the same meaning. We are most familiar with confession, but because I prefer to have each principle begin with the letter "p", I will use profession.

Promise Fulfillment

When God makes a promise, you can trust Him to keep it. Hebrews 10:23 (KJV) confirms that, it says we should *"... hold fast the profession of our faith without wavering; (for he is faithful that promised;)"*. There's no question about God's role in promise fulfillment. He watches over every Word He speaks to make sure it comes to pass Jer. 1:12 (NASU). Let me reiterate, He can be trusted, but there's a role that we have in promise fulfillment too. Our participation is required. Correct scriptural interpretation reveals the promises of God are received by the law of faith. (Rom. 3:27) However, it is through the spiritual action of profession that the manifestation of what's hoped for is ultimately received.

Faith is apparent by what is spoken out of the mouth and what is believed in the heart. Rom 10:8-9 says, *"... The word is nigh thee, even in thy mouth, and in thy heart: that is, the word of faith, which we preach; That if thou shalt confess with thy mouth the Lord Jesus, and shalt believe in thine heart that God hath raised him from the dead, thou shalt be saved."* Here, Paul is talking about faith for salvation, but it is the same kind of faith that is required to bring to pass every promise of God. Faith must be in your heart and in your mouth. If both aren't working together at the same time, then faith will not work! Faith comes by hearing, but it's realized by what is said and believed. There is a definite connection between what is said out of the mouth and what is experienced in life.

> Faith comes by hearing, but it's realized by what is said and believed.

God spoke to my heart and said, "If we're going to experience the manifestation of the promises of God, we must learn how to control our mouths." So, the question is: How is the mouth controlled? The mouth is brought under control by: 1) Understanding the creative power of words; 2) Guarding the words that come out of the mouth; and 3) Allowing God to Tame the Tongue.

Creative Power of Words

Do you realize that you go through life with a remarkable power, a power that is equivalent to fire, electricity, or even nuclear energy? And get this, it is right under your nose. It's a power so great that it's capable of producing life and death, depending on how it is used. The Bible tells us, our words are so powerful that they can encourage or discourage... hurt or heal... tear down or build up. Our words can influence the way we act and feel and determine our attitude and outlook on life. Proverbs

IT'S YOUR TURN NOW!

18:21 reminds us: *"Death and life are in the power of the tongue: and they that love it shall eat the fruit thereof."*

Words have creative power. And just like God used His Words to create the world, your words also have the power to create your world. Before God spoke, the world was in total confusion. It was without form, empty and full of darkness. His spoken Word brought order in the midst of chaos and confusion, and created what he desired. What did He desire? Nine different times in Genesis chapter 1, God spoke what He desired. When He spoke, the power that was in His Words created His desires. Genesis says, He saw what He said and it was good, and even, very good!

What do you desire? Is your world in total confusion? Is your life empty? Is there darkness and disorder all around you? You have the power to change it! Ephesians 5:1 holds the key: *"Imitate God, therefore, in everything you do, because you are his dear children"* (NLT). That's right, imitate God! Copy Him! God never spoke what He saw. On the contrary, He spoke what He wanted to see. He saw darkness, but He spoke light; He saw disorder, but He spoke order. He only spoke what He desired to see and as a result, His words changed the entire world. And you, my sister, must do what He did. Only speak words that are in agreement with what you desire. When we consistently speak faith-filled words without wavering, they will create our world too, and it will be very good!

> Only speak words that are in agreement with what you desire.

ALMA GORDON BAMBERG

Watch Your Mouth

"Then those who feared the Lord talked often one to another, and the Lord listened and heard it, and a book of remembrance was written before Him of those who reverenced and worshipfully feared the Lord and who thought on His name" Mal 3:16 (Amplified). Can God record your conversations in His Book of Remembrance? Whether you realize it or not, He's listening to every word you say. That's why it's very important to watch what you say. Psalm 141:3 (KJV) says, *"Set a watch, O Lord, before my mouth; keep the door of my lips."* The Living Bible says, *"Help me, Lord, to keep my mouth shut and my Lips sealed."* I believe the mouth has the potential of getting us in trouble more than any other member of our bodies.

> The degree of faith can be measured, oftentimes, by the words spoken during difficult times.

The word *watch* means to guard, look after, keep an eye on, mind, or to have a watchdog mentality. Based on the previous scripture, a watchdog mentality is required when it comes to the words that come out of the mouth. There is a need to stand guard against negative faithless words. The degree of faith can be measured, oftentimes, by the words spoken during difficult times. You might be surprised by what you hear when trouble arises, because your words will locate your faith. There's no question about it, when you are extremely emotional – either good or bad – it's easy to say just what you're feeling. It's sometimes difficult to say right things when you feel totally wrong. But in those moments, it's important to allow faith to rise above emotions and speak in agreement with God's Word and what you truly believe and not what you feel. Losing your temper and venting your frustration through angry words can lead to bitter grief, torment and can even ruin relationships.

If you are facing difficulties in your life, this will be a good time to take inventory of what and how you speak. It would be wise to discipline your mouth by using self-control. Eph. 4:29-30 says, *"Let no foul or polluting language, nor evil word nor unwholesome or worthless talk [ever] come out of your mouth, but only such [speech] as is good and beneficial to the spiritual progress of others, as is fitting to the need and the occasion, that it may be a blessing and give grace (God's favor) to those who hear it"* (Amplified). If you want to discipline your mouth it's not enough to just stop talking negatively. You must replace those negative, faithless words, with positive, faith-filled words. The cliché that says, "If you can't say anything nice don't say anything at all," is not for the believer. If you say nothing, you have nothing. Mark 11:23 says, *"...That whosoever shall say unto this mountain, ...and shall not doubt in his heart, but shall believe that those things which he saith shall come to pass; he shall have whatsoever he saith."*

Are you suffering from a heart condition? The condition of the heart determines the fruit of your lips, so make sure you work on your heart first. Ask God to create in you a clean heart and renew the right spirit within you (Ps. 51:10). Matthew 12:34-37 is clear, what's in the heart comes out of the mouth: *"O generation of vipers, how can ye, being evil, speak good things? for out of the abundance of the heart the mouth speaketh. A good man out of the good treasure of the heart bringeth forth good things: and an evil man out of the evil treasure bringeth forth evil things. But I say unto you, That every idle word that men shall speak, they shall give account thereof in the day of judgment. For by thy words thou shalt be justified, and by thy words thou shalt be condemned."* The choice of words you speak is yours, choose wisely.

God, Tame My Tongue

"...The tongue is a little member, and it can boast of great things. See how much wood or how great a forest a tiny spark can set ablaze! And the tongue is a fire [The tongue is a] world of wickedness set among our members, contaminating and depraving the whole body and setting on fire the wheel of birth (the cycle of man's nature), being itself ignited by hell. For every kind of beast and bird, of reptile and sea animal, can be tamed and has been tamed by human genius (nature). But the human tongue can be tamed by no man. It is a restless (undisciplined, irreconcilable) evil, full of deadly poison" (James chapter 3:5-12). Man is able to tame wild animals of the jungle but no man can tame the tongue. The tongue is destructive and undisciplined. It has the power to contaminate and corrupt your entire life. It takes the help of the Holy Spirit to save you from the destructive power of your own

words. The tongue has to be trained on purpose to speak the words that will produce victory in your life.

Personal Profession Regimen

In July 2014 my biological sisters and I took my parents on an Orlando, Florida vacation. Early one morning, as everyone slept, I decided to go out on the balcony to read. As I sat there meditating on what I had just read, a barrage of thoughts concerning my current state in life, flooded my mind. I began thinking about where I was at that point in my life. I thought about where I was and imagined where I wanted to be. I envisioned what I wanted most out of life and who I wanted to share my life with. And suddenly, I knew I was at the threshold of a new season of life. There were no trumpets blaring in my ears, no audible voice from heaven, no, none of that. It was just "a knowing" in my spirit that something was changing for me. I remember thinking, God is about to do something new in my life and it would require my participation.

Without hesitation and much effort, I began writing what I had envisioned. I ended up writing eight personal confessions about who I wanted to become; what I want to have; where I wanted to go in life and how it all affected the people in my life. If you understand numerology, you would agree with me that it was no accident that I ended up with eight statements about myself. You see, the number eight in the Bible is the number of "new beginnings." *"It signifies resurrection and regeneration. Eight is also associated with the beginning of a new era or a new order"* [6]. I was on the brink of something new in my life but it wasn't automatic. I had to do something. Because I have been created to function like my heavenly Father and I understood the principle of profession, I made a commitment to include those eight confessions in my daily spiritual regimen. I knew if I was going to experience the change God wanted for me, I had to engage my mouth. I had to start speaking out what I saw on the inside. And from that day until now, I have professed daily my personal confessions and held fast to my commitment without wavering, knowing God is faithful who promised. With that in mind, I'd like to share with you my personal professions of faith about myself:

1) *Right NOW,* I am a cool, calm, collected, creative, confident woman, wife, entrepreneur, leader, transformational speaker/teacher/preacher, and bestselling author who is smart and intellectually astute.
   Why? Because I desire:
   - Emotional balance;
   - My imagination and artistic abilities to flow freely and unhindered in every area of my life;
   - To be a wise cutting-edge thought leader.

2) *Right NOW,* my mind/soul, body and spirit is perfectly synchronized and maximizes all God-given functions according to design.
   Why? Because I desire:
   - A healthy well-balanced long life;

IT'S YOUR TURN NOW!

- Every part of my being to function harmoniously.

3) *Right NOW,* my life is filled, full, and overlowing with purpose, passion, and realized potential.
   Why? <u>Because I desire</u>:
   - To be and do all I was created to be and do;
   - To finish what I was called to the planet to do;
   - To die empty.

4) *Right NOW,* the overflow from my life is freely given to others in abundance without hesitation and reservation with balance.
   Why? <u>Because I desire</u>:
   - To be a blessing to others;
   - To be a blessing to the kingdom of God.

5) *Right NOW,* my husband does safely trust in me and we enjoy each other's company; I joyfully do him good all the days of our lives.
   Why? <u>Because I desire</u>:
   - A great marital relationship;
   - Our marriage to be a godly example to others.

6) *Right NOW,* _____(spouse's name) and I are financially wealthy, and all of our needs are supplied and all of our desires are granted.
   Why? <u>Because I desire</u>:
   - Freedom from burdensome debt;
   - Financial stability;

- To support the kingdom of God;
- To support my parents and family;
- To leave an inheritance for future generations;
- To travel the world and enjoy the abundant life Jesus came to give me.

7) *Right NOW,* _____(spouse's name) and I embrace every age and stage of life with zest and vitality with expectation of not only quantity of days, but quality of life.

   Why? <u>Because I desire</u>:
   - To live with hope and contentment at all times;
   - To live a first-class lifestyle.

8) *Right NOW,* healthy eating habits, exercise and proper rest are a part of my daily routine and reverses all generational sickness, disease and dis-ease.

   Why? <u>Because I desire</u>:
   - To be free from the inordinate and excessive control of medication and doctors appointments;
   - To be physically fit to carry out my assignments and to fulfill my purpose.

I believe how you see yourself and what you say about yourself is vitally important! The way you talk to and about yourself makes all the difference in being prepared to take your turn. I urge you to take responsibility for your words. Allow the Holy Spirit to use the Word of God to tame your tongue. Ask God to help you by praying daily Psalms 19:14 (KJV). *"Let the words of my mouth,*

IT'S YOUR TURN NOW!

and the meditation of my heart, be acceptable in thy sight, O LORD, my strength, and my redeemer."

ALMA GORDON BAMBERG

IT'S YOUR TURN NOW TO WORK ON YOU

Self-Reflection Exercise:

Ask yourself –

1) What do I want, desire and envision for my life?
   _____
   _____

2) What am I saying about my life? *(Can God record my conversations in His Book of Remembrance?)*
   _____
   _____

3) If I measured the degree of my faith by my recent conversations, how would I measure up? *(Little faith? Great faith? Strong faith? or No faith?)*
   _____
   _____

4) Have I been engaging in negative talk and conversations? If I have, what faith-filled words should I replace them with? _____
   _____
   _____

5) What are my Personal Professions of Faith about myself? _____
   _____

IT'S YOUR TURN NOW!

CHAPTER 12

My Position

Answers the question: WHERE? INFLUENCE?

"The king loved Esther more than all the other women, and she obtained grace and favor in his sight more than all the virgins; so he set the royal crown upon her head and made her queen instead of Vashti" (Esther 2:17 NKJV). *"Who knows if perhaps you were made **queen** for just such a time as this?"* (Esther 4:14)

Wakeup Call

Position answers the question of where will you use your influence. During Mordecai's and Esther's discourse, he sharply addressed her purpose for being in the position of queen. He said *"Do not think in your heart that you will escape in the king's palace any more than all the other Jews. For if you remain completely silent at this time, relief and deliverance will arise for the Jews from another place, but you and your father's house will perish. Yet who knows whether you have come to the kingdom for such a time as this?"* (Esther 4:13-14 NKJV) Let me interpret Mordecai's response in Bam-language. He sharply reprimanded her and said, "Esther, don't you get the big head. If you don't help us, God will raise up a deliverer from somewhere else. But know this, you and your family will die! Don't forget, you're walking around acting like all the other Persian virgins, but let me remind you who you really are. You are a Jew! You'll be seen as a perpetrator! Don't you forget, for the past nine years, your nationality has been kept a secret. But when they find out who you are, you and your whole family will die! Think about it Esther! Just maybe the purpose for which you hold that royal position is for this very reason."

We can see how Esther needed a wakeup call, but what about you? What is the purpose for the position you hold? How are you using your influential position to help others?

Position of Influence

Esther eventually realized the royal position she held was for the purpose of using her influence to change legislation that would ultimately rescue a nation from extinction. Esther's newfound position in the Kingdom was very powerful. It afforded her influence that she would not have otherwise had. Esther was planted in a pagan palace so she could use her power of influence over a king to spare her people from ethnic cleansing. Her influence literally impacted the trajectory of an entire nation. No military intervention was required. No revolution needed. Just one woman submitted to the plan and purposes of God who understood the power of her position. Do you understand the power of your position or influence *you* possess? Do *you* know it has the potential to impact the trajectory of others just like Esther?

ALMA GORDON BAMBERG

Every woman has influence. She has been given it to affect good and not evil. She must never use it as a form of manipulation to get her own way but for the good of others. Even the pagan politicians knew that women had influence. That's why Esther's predecessor, Vashti, was dethroned after digging her heels in against the king's request. Why? Because the other men also understood her position alone had the ability to influence their wives to behave just like she behaved.

The Bible says, you too, have a royal position of influence. We operate in the position of a royal priesthood: *"But ye are a chosen generation, a royal priesthood, a holy nation, a peculiar people; that ye should shew forth the praises of him who hath called you out of darkness into his marvellous light"* 1 Peter 2:9. We are the King's priest. We have been called to this royal position to use our influence on behalf of others. Where have you been positioned in the kingdom of God to use your position of influence? Perhaps your position of influence is to help mothers, wives, singles, entrepreneurs, professionals in the corporate arena or ministry to young teenage mothers? Or, maybe it's in the school system, government, service industry or sales? We have all been given a powerful position of influence. Whoever you are, wherever you are in life, you are a woman of influence. The question for you and I is, how will we use our position to influence others? Will we use it for selfish gain or will we understand the influential power given to us

> Whoever you are, wherever you are in life, you are a woman of influence.

was God-given to advance the cause of someone who is unable to help or speak for themselves?

Blessed and Highly Favored

We all want favor. Defining ourselves as highly favored has become a commonly used response to the question, "How are you?" To which some respond, "I'm blessed and highly favored." But the true test of favor, extended to any of us, lies in our willingness to use what we've been given, in this case, our position(s) of influence, to help others. The favor showed to Esther extended far beyond herself to a people who couldn't speak for themselves. This is truly what it means to be blessed and highly favored. So, let me ask you, "Are you blessed and highly favored?"

No Fairytale Princess

Today's society is totally obsessed with exterior beauty and sexuality. From the moment some baby girls enter the world, they are conditioned to believe happiness and success is the result of their outward appearance. Young mothers pride themselves in dressing their daughters like a baby doll or their mini-me, adorning them in the latest women's fads and fashions. Most of us, as young girls spent our childhood days eager to be the latest Disney princess that lived in a palace and married the prince. We were attracted to the beautiful glistening gown and the rhinestone studded tiara of the stunning young lady who always ended up with the handsome prince saving the day and living happily ever after.

Esther's story was not the latest and greatest Disney princess fairytale told for our entertainment. Instead, it was a true account of an ordinary Jewish young lady who had been elevated to the position of queen of the Persian Empire. Who, by no choice of her own, was chosen to exemplify an uncommon degree of courage to rescue a Jewish nation from certain annihilation. Taken into captivity, nationality sworn to secrecy and introduced into a culture that was unfamiliar to everything and everyone she ever knew. She remained faithful to her call, a call that could have very well costed her, her life. But in the face of certain death, she came to the realization that becoming queen and saving her people was the purpose for which she had been chosen. In fact, this was the purpose for which she had been born. Her courageous choice to deny any selfish desires that she might have felt to rescue a people who could in no wise save themselves, continues to teach us life altering lessons that have lasted for thousands of years.

We can read Esther's story and assume it was all about her receiving favor and getting to a seat of power and influence by becoming the queen of Persia. But the truth of the matter is, Esther's defining moment rested in her willingness to use her position of favor and influence to bring deliverance and freedom to a people who needed her help.

IT'S YOUR TURN NOW!

IT'S YOUR TURN NOW TO WORK ON YOU

Self-Reflection Exercise:

Ask yourself –

1) What position(s) of influence do I *currently* hold?

_____
_____
_____
_____

2) Who does my influence most impact? Who needs my help? _____

_____
_____

3) What person or people am I being challenged to use my position of influence to help? Why?

_____
_____
_____
_____
_____

CHAPTER 13

My Price

Answers the question of: COST? What PRICE are you Willing to PAY?

"Go and gather together all the Jews of Susa and fast for me. Do not eat or drink for three days, night or day. My maids and I will do the same. And then, though it is against the law, I will go in to see the king. If I must die, I must die." – Esther 4:13-14 (NLT)

Willing to Pay the Price?

Price answers the question of COST? How much are you willing to pay? When going into a department store and spotting an item you'd like to buy, do you look at the price tag before you purchase it? Why do you do that? I know why I look at the price tag, I want to know if I'm willing to pay the price. Have you ever said, I really like that outfit but I'm not going to pay "that price" for it? When I think about the blessings, God has in store for us, oftentimes, we have the same mindset. We want the blessings of God but when we examine the cost of our time, talent and/or treasure, we often say, I'm unwilling to pay the price. As long as we maintain that mentality, we'll never wear the blessings, we'll

IT'S YOUR TURN NOW!

never experience the blessings, and we'll never enjoy the blessings.

Undercover Queen's Defining Moment

In the twelfth year of the king's reign, Haman, the enemy of the Jews got fed up with Mordecai not bowing down to him. He saw it as disrespect so he sought ways to get rid of him. After finding out Mordecai was a Jew he wasn't content with just killing him but he sought to destroy the whole Jewish nation. He devised a plan to deceive the king into signing a decree to destroy the Jewish Nation knowing the law could not be reversed.

Meanwhile, Mordecai and the entire Jewish nation is in mourning over this new law. He's sitting in the city square with his clothes torn, covered in ashes and crying out in a loud bitter cry. Esther gets word and is afraid her cover will be blown. She sends one of the palace assistants to Mordecai to find out what's going on. He shares the law and sends a message to her to go before the king to ask for relief for the Jewish nation. Esther responded by sharing another law. She tells him, there is a law that says anyone who goes into the inner court who hasn't been called by the king, would surely be put to death except he holds out the scepter. She further explains, it's been thirty days since the king last called her.

All these years Esther had not revealed her nationality. She had spent the first four years preparing to go before the King to *win* the influence of the position. And for the next five years she prepared to go before the King to *use* the influence of her position to help others. It was a total of nine years of preparation for this very moment. Esther's turn had come to face her most crucial test of faith. Just picture Esther walking around the palace as an undercover Jew because Mordecai had given her strict instructions to keep her nationality a secret *until* the appointed time. Well, the appointed time had come. This was her defining moment. Will she step up and take her turn? Will she demonstrate whether or not she truly understood the purpose for which she had been placed in that position of influence and authority? What will she do?

The Price of Courage

There is a cost associated with taking your turn and it's far greater than any amount of money. It's the price of overcoming your fears. When Esther heard of the decree to annihilate the Jewish nation, the Bible says she *"was seized by great fear"* (Esther 4:4 AMP). Fear comes to intimidate you. It dares you to move. Fear tells you, "You better NOT try that! Who do you think you are? You know you don't have enough money to do that. You don't have enough help; enough education; enough skill; enough know how. It tells you, you know you're getting older and your health is failing. You're not as strong as you used to be or as smart as you used to be." It reminds you of every failure you've ever had and assaults your mind in an effort to paralyze you depriving you of movement and bringing you to a complete stop! I've been there!

> Courage is not the absence of fear, but the ability to face the fear and do it anyway.

IT'S YOUR TURN NOW!

So, how do you overcome fear? Whenever fear is present, courage is required. Courage is not the absence of fear, but the ability to face the fear and do it anyway. Honestly, the only way courage can be demonstrated is in the presence of fear. Esther faced her fears. She was courageous. She was determined to see the king even if it costs her life. She made up in her mind she was willing to pay the price. Despite the law and legislation of the land, she rose up in the face of certain death and declared, *"If I perish, I perish,"* but I am going to do what God has ordained for my life. She was fully aware that the king had not sent for her but she made up in her mind *"I am going to see the King"* anyway. Esther paid the price and faced her fears. Will you pay the price to face yours?

Purpose Found in a Problem

Is it possible to find your purpose in your problem? Could it be that your purpose is hiding out in your problem? Esther found her purpose in a problem. She had come this far by her faith in Jehovah and was fully prepared to die for what she believed.

When it actually came time for Esther to save her people, look at the passion in which she spoke to the king: "... *"If it pleases the king, and if I have found favor in his sight and the thing seems right to the king and I am pleasing in his eyes, let it be written to revoke the letters devised by Haman, ... which he wrote to annihilate the Jews who are in all the king's provinces. For how can I endure to see the evil that will come to my people? Or how can I endure to see the destruction of my countrymen?"* (Esther 8:4b-6). I can just imagine the tears rolling down her cheeks. I can feel her agony. Unable to endure or bear the thought of her people being destroyed, she couldn't remain silent any longer. She was determined to speak up! She realized the law demanded her death and she was willing to die! (Esther 4:16) Now, that's purpose!

Purpose is finding that "thing" for which you are willing to die for. Purpose is finding that cause, that vision, that idea, that "thing" that you are willing to put everything on the line for, even your life. It reminds me of something David said when he was confronted about his drive to kill Goliath, the Philistine giant, who was taunting the army of the living God. *"...David's oldest brother, Eliab, heard David talking to the men, he got angry. "What are you doing around here anyway?" he demanded. "What about those few sheep you're supposed to be taking care of?"* (1 Samuel 17:28 NLT) He accused David of just wanting to come out to the see the battle. He insinuated that David was just a child and being on the battle front was beyond his years and capability. But David boldly stood up, took his turn and asked a question that still reverberates for thousands of years: *"...Is there not a cause?"* (1 Samuel 17:29 KJV) David found his CAUSE.

> "If you haven't found something you're willing to die for, you aren't fit to live."
> -Martin Luther King Jr.

He found that "thing" that he was not only willing to live for but to die for. Do you have something you believe in so strongly that

IT'S YOUR TURN NOW!

you're willing to die for it? Martin Luther King, Jr. said, *"If you haven't found something you're willing to die for, you aren't fit to live."*

Courage Under Fire

I must warn you, when you make a decision to take your turn, expect your courage to be constantly under attack. It's the job of Satan, your enemy to steal, kill and destroy every ounce of faith you possess. He wants to intimidate you. But take courage, God has given you everything you need to overcome the spirit of fear (2 Timothy 1:7). You don't have to allow fear to dominate your life. God has already provided you with adequate miracle working power to overcome all the power of the enemy.

Luke, the New Testament physician, further explains what this power can do. *"Behold, I give unto you power to tread on serpents and scorpions, and over all the power of the enemy: and nothing shall by any means hurt you."* (Luke 10:19 KJV). The first word "power" in that verse in its original Greek rendering is the word exousia (ex-oo-see'-ah)[7]. It has to do with exercising jurisdictional authority over another. It has to do with bringing a lesser power under the power of another who is greater. It's delegated influence. In other words, you have been given authorization to act as a representative of God's power. You have been deputized to act on behalf of the one who has all power. You have been given a higher position of power than the power the enemy has. You outrank him. He's always beneath you. He's under your foot.

If Satan has been threatening you to the point where you're seized with great fear, and your courage is under fire, allow Esther's story to teach you how to handle it. She exemplified uncommon courage.

> Courage is the ability to face danger, difficulty, and uncertainty without being overcome by fear to the degree that it deflects and derails you from your God-ordained course of action.

She demonstrated the ability to face danger, difficulty, and certain death without being overcome by fear to the degree that it deflected and derailed her from her God-ordained course of action. She faced her fear and courageously took her turn. You too, must be willing to face your fears and pay whatever price you must pay knowing, *"...God hath not given you the spirit of fear; but of power, and of love, and of a sound mind"* 2 Timothy 1:7 (KJV).

IT'S YOUR TURN NOW!

IT'S YOUR TURN NOW TO WORK ON YOU

Self-Reflection Exercise:

Ask yourself –

1) What fear tactics am I being confronted with?
   _____
   _____
   _____

2) What do I need to do when my courage is under attack? *(What do I need to do to overcome my fear(s)? How do I handle intimidating thoughts of failure?)* _____
   _____
   _____
   _____

3) What price am I willing to pay to face my fears? *(i.e. time, talent, treasure, comfort, friendships, etc)*
   _____
   _____
   _____

4) What am I willing to die for? _____
   _____
   _____

CHAPTER 14

My Promotion

Answers the Question of: REWARD?

"Then Esther went again before the king, ... Esther said, "If it please the king, and if I have found favor with him, and if he thinks it is right, and if I am pleasing to him, let there be a decree that reverses the orders of Haman ... who ordered that Jews throughout all the king's provinces should be destroyed (Esther 8:3a;5 NLT). *Then King Ahasuerus said to Queen Esther and Mordecai the Jew, "Indeed, I have given Esther the house of Haman, and they have hanged him on the gallows because he tried to lay his hand on the Jews. You yourselves write a decree concerning the Jews, as you please, in the king's name, and seal it with the king's signet ring; for whatever is written in the king's name and sealed with the king's signet ring no one can revoke"* (Esther 8:7-8 NKJV).

Prerequisite for Promotion

If you prepare yourself NOW, it won't be long before God promotes you. Wikipedia's etymology and usage of the term, promotion means to "move forward", "push onward", or to "advance in rank or position". God spoke these words to me, *"Preparation is the prerequisite for promotion"* – Alma Bamberg.

IT'S YOUR TURN NOW!

If you submit yourself to God's preparation process and consistently apply the principles in your life, you can expect promotion.

Esther prepared herself and won the heart of the king. In fact, he favored her so much that he was willing to give her up to half of the kingdom before she made her request. Esther didn't immediately make her request known, she was a woman of great *patience*. She was willing to wait for the "set time." God had given her a *plan* and she was poised and self-controlled enough to maintain her *position* in every phase of the plan. She understood her *time* and seasons and would not allow anyone or anything to derail her from it.

The king asked her the second time, "Esther, what do you want?" This time, God said, "Esther, it's your turn now, to speak up." This time, she boldly said, *"...If I have found favor in your sight, O king, and if it pleases the king, let my life be given me at **my** petition, and **my** people at **my** request. For we have been sold, my people and I, to be destroyed, to be killed, and to be annihilated..."* (Esther 7:3-4).

The king responded with total disgust and anger that anyone would want to kill the queen. His anger was so enraged that it could not be satisfied until the one who had devised such a wicked plan would die in the same manner in which he had

> *"For promotion cometh neither from the east, nor from the west, nor from the south. But God is the judge: he putteth down one, and setteth up another."*
> Ps. 75:6-7 KJV

devised for Queen Esther and her people. That day, Haman, the enemy of the Jews lost his property, his position of authority, and most of all his life. And guess who replaced him? The very one Haman most despised, Mordecai. Don't tell me what God will not do!!! Psalm 75:6-7 KJV says, *"For promotion cometh neither from the east, nor from the west, nor from the south. But God is the judge: he putteth down one, and setteth up another."* He has a way of causing you to replace the very person who has despitefully used you, and said all manner of evil against you. I'm telling you, sometimes, God's promotions come in the most unlikely way.

A Higher Law

There's no doubt about it, in the Persian Kingdom, whenever there was a law that had been written in the king's name and sealed with the king's signet ring, it could never be revoked. Esther's request to reverse the law set in motion by Haman could not be reversed. How could the king help Esther now? Was there anything he could do? There was nothing that could be done *except* for the king to write a higher law. A law that superseded the law initiated by Haman that forced it out of use and made it inferior and ineffective.

The law of gravity and the law of lift as it relates to an airplane's ability to fly is a great example of what transpired when Esther and Mordecai wrote a higher law. The law of gravity says, what goes up must come down. So, how is it that an airplane is able to fly? The law of lift supersedes the law of gravity. *"Lift is*

IT'S YOUR TURN NOW!

the force that directly opposes the weight of an airplane and holds the airplane in the air. Lift is generated by every part of the airplane, but most of the lift on a normal airliner is generated by the wings. Lift is a mechanical aerodynamic force produced by the motion of the airplane through the air." [8] As long as the law of lift is enforced, the law of gravity doesn't go away, it's just becomes ineffective. The law of lift has a greater force over gravity. So, it is, with the power Jesus spoke of in Luke 10:19. The power you and I have been given supersedes any power the enemy has against us and whatever he throws our way will not harm us. His power is real, it's just been rendered ineffective when you enforce the power God over the power of the enemy.

Legislative Law Enforcement Agents

"Then King Ahasuerus said to Queen Esther and Mordecai the Jew, "Indeed, I have given Esther the house of Haman, ... ⁸ You yourselves write a decree concerning the Jews, as you please, in the king's name, and seal it with the king's signet ring; for whatever is written in the king's name and sealed with the king's signet ring no one can revoke" (Esther 8:7-8 NKJV). Esther and Mortdecai had been granted authority to write new legislation affecting the Jews in all the providences, however they saw fit to write it. They would then seal it with the king's signet ring, which meant it could not be revoked. Look at how God promoted an orphan girl and a despised Jewish man to the top legislative position in a Persian government.

The new law written by Mordecai *"... gave the Jews in every city authority to unite to defend their lives. They were allowed to kill, slaughter, and annihilate anyone of any nationality or province who might attack them or their children and wives, and to take the property of their enemies".* (Esther 8:11). A copy of the document was issued as a decree in every province and published for all people, so that the Jews would be ready to avenge themselves on their enemies." (Esther 8:13 NKJV). *"In every province and city, wherever the king's decree arrived, the Jews rejoiced and had a great celebration and declared a public festival and holiday. And many of the people of the land became Jews themselves, for they feared what the Jews might do to them."* (Esther 8:17)

Authority Granted

The final chapters of Esther's story closed with Esther not only positively affecting legislation to stop the destruction of her people, but she, along with Mordecai, was given full authority of the office of the king. They were given permission to pen new legislation that benefitted the good of the Jewish people.

How incredible it was that Esther was willing to die to save a nation of people! The very thing that looked like it would take Esther under, took her higher and elevated her to a position of the highest legislative power. She couldn't understand how she could come out victorious with both the Jewish people and the Persian King. But in the end, she won the heart of both! Her husband safely trusted in her judgment, so much that she was allowed to make legislative decisions that impacted not only her people, but an entire Persian Empire!

Esther was a woman who knew her purpose. She knew she was called to the palace to save the nation of Israel from annihilation. She was willing to fulfill that purpose, even in the face of danger and certain death. Will the same be said of you?

A Long Time Coming

One morning, I was watching Good Morning America (GMA) when the movie, "Fences" had just come out. Denzel Washington, the Oscar Winner who directed and starred in the movie, was interviewed by Michael Strahan. He was asked about the role of Viola Davis. "What have you learned from her that makes her so special?" Almost lost for words, Denzel finally responded and I quote, "She's just one of those rare actors and it's her turn now…it's her turn. You know, she's been good a long time but now everybody has caught up with her and now she's getting the recognition she deserves."

As I come to the close of this book, I'd like to address those of you who have been waiting on promotion or the fulfillment of a promise for what you might call a long time. Your confidence is somewhat shaken and you're contemplating whether or not you have the strength to hold on and keep going. There's a great reward waiting on you if you will patiently maintain your confidence in God, knowing He's preparing you for something greater. Don't allow discouragement to cause you to throw in the towel and give up now. Hang in there.

The book of Hebrews encourages us by saying *"Cast not away therefore your confidence, which hath great recompense of reward. For ye have need of patience, that, after ye have done the will of God, ye might receive the promise."* Hebrews 10:34-36 (KJV)

I love the words of the Message Bible: *"Remember those early days after you first saw the light? Those were the hard times! Kicked around in public, targets of every kind of abuse—some days it was you, other days your friends. If some friends went to prison, you stuck by them. If some enemies broke in and seized your goods, you let them go with a smile, knowing they couldn't touch your real treasure. Nothing they did bothered you, nothing set you back. So, don't throw it all away now. You were sure of yourselves then. It's still a sure thing! But you need to stick it out, staying with God's plan so you'll be there for the promised completion. It won't be long now, he's on the way; he'll show up most any minute. But anyone who is right with me thrives on loyal trust; if he cuts and runs, I won't be very happy. But we're not quitters who lose out. Oh, no! We'll stay with it and survive, trusting all the way."* (Heb. 10:32-39 MSG)

> **"So, don't throw it all away now. You were sure of yourselves then. It's still a sure thing! But you need to stick it out, staying with God's plan so you'll be there for the promised completion."**
> -Hebrews 10:35-36 (MSG)

IT'S YOUR TURN NOW!

Please don't throw everything you've worked for away now, not after all you've been through. Don't quit. Stick with the plan and purpose God has for your life. The enemy of your soul, Satan, will do everything he can to cause you to quit. But if you quit now, you will certainly lose out on the fulfillment of what God promised you. Galatians 6:9-10 (AMPC) says, *"And let us not lose heart and grow weary and faint in acting nobly and doing right, for in due time and at the appointed season we shall reap, if we do not loosen and relax our courage and faint. So then, as occasion and opportunity open up to us, let us do good [morally] to all people [not only being useful or profitable to them, but also doing what is for their spiritual good and advantage]. Be mindful to be a blessing, especially to those of the household of faith [those who belong to God's family with you, the believers]."*

Your turn might be a long time coming, and others may not recognize what makes you so special, but a day will come when you will get what you deserve. God sees, and He knows when it's your turn.

IT'S YOUR TURN NOW TO WORK ON YOU

Self-Reflection Exercise:

Ask yourself –

1) What promotion am I expecting or desiring?
   _____
   _____

2) How will my promotion affect change in the lives of others? *(benefit others?)*
   _____
   _____

3) How does the power of God working in my life give me an advantage?
   _____
   _____

4) What promotion(s) have I dismissed based on my own perceived inadequacies and/or flaws?
   _____
   _____

5) What limitations have I placed on myself when God has removed the limits and opened the door for promotion?
   _____
   _____

SECTION V

The Prayer of Preparation

CHAPTER 15

God's Ultimate Plan for You

The Plan of Salvation

Some of you may not believe God's thinking about you, but really, He is. He simply adores you and wants the very best for you. The Psalmist said, *"What is man, that thou art mindful of him?"* (Ps. 8:4 KJV). The Easy-to-Read Version says, *"I look at the heavens you made with your hands. I see the moon and the stars you created. And I wonder, "Why are people so important to you? Why do you even think about them? Why do you care so much about humans? Why do you even notice them?" But you made them almost like gods and crowned them with glory and honor."* Psalm 8:3-5 (ERV)

Now, that is a powerful scripture text! To know that Jehovah God, the Great I AM, is taking notice of you! To know that you are so important to Him that He would make you in His likeness

IT'S YOUR TURN NOW!

and in His image, is incredible! And you might ask, "Why is He thinking about You?" First of all, you're on His mind because He desires a personal relationship with you as your heavenly Father. He loves you. God so loved you that He gave His only Son to die in your place so that you can live in eternity with Him.

The prophet Jeremiah said, God has been thinking about the plans He has for you, *"plans to prosper you and not to harm you, plans to give you hope and a future."* Jeremiah 29:11 (NIV). You see, His plan for you extends way beyond your lifetime here on earth into eternity. It's called the plan of salvation. God's universal plan of salvation is to adopt you into His family and that adoption is based on His love for you and what He has done for you through Jesus Christ. 1 John 3:1 (AMP) makes it clear that this is "an incredible quality of love the Father has shown to us, that we would [be permitted to] be named and called and counted the children of God!" And get this, there's nothing you've done in your past that could make Him reject you. He knows everything there is to know about you and He still accepts you. Perhaps you're feeling unworthy. God's love for you is not based on your worth but on His grace. It is an amazing grace!

> God's love for you is not based on your worth but on His grace. It is an AMAZING GRACE!

I want you to know, as long as there's breath in your body, our heavenly Father has you on His mind. He desires nothing less than His best for you. He doesn't want any harm to come to you. He has a glorious future planned for you, and He's waiting to show it to you. All you have to do is accept it by accepting what His Son, Jesus Christ has done for you.

How do you accept Jesus into your life? You must first recognize that you are a sinner in need of a Savior. (Romans 3:23) God desires perfection and you cannot meet that requirement on your own merits. Therefore, out of His love, God came down in the flesh and personhood of Jesus. He lived a perfect life. He lived the life you couldn't live and paid the price you couldn't pay. He died, He was buried, and He was resurrected for your sins. Now, all you have to do is to repent of your sins and trust that what Christ has done for you is enough. Jesus is the only way. (John 14:6) Open up your heart and invite Him in today. It's your turn now to let Him in.

If you are ready, pray God's Plan of Salvation written below: Heavenly Father, I acknowledge any sin I have committed against You or my fellowman, in my thoughts, words, deeds, or actions. Forgive me of my sins and transgressions. Father, I confess with my mouth and believe in my heart that Jesus died and rose again, that I might receive forgiveness and have eternal life. Thank you, Jesus, for redeeming my life from destruction. Holy Spirit, I invite You into my heart. Fill me with the baptism of the Holy Spirit. Lead me, guide me, direct me, and bring to my remembrance the things God requires of me. In Jesus Name, AMEN!

IT'S YOUR TURN NOW!

IT'S YOUR TURN NOW TO WORK ON YOU

Self-Reflection Exercise:

Ask yourself –

1) Have I accepted Jesus as Lord and Savior of my life?
   _____
   _____

2) What is preventing me from repenting or asking forgiveness?
   _____
   _____

3) Do I trust and believe what Christ has done for me in His death, burial and resurrection is enough to pay the price for my sins?
   _____
   _____

4) Have I opened up my heart and invite Jesus in?
   _____
   _____

5) Have I confessed the Prayer of Salvation? If not, Why?
   _____
   _____

ALMA GORDON BAMBERG

CHAPTER 16

My Prayer for You

All of us need help. The Holy Spirit, who is our helper, standby, and comforter is present to help you right where you are. Jesus said in the book of John that He would pray to His Father, and God the Father, would give you another comforter who would abide with you forever. John 14:16 (KJV). He's willing to aide and support you. He will do for you what you can't do for yourself. I simply want to join my faith with yours in a prayer of agreement for God's best for your life. Let's pray.

Father, behold my sisters. We need YOU! We come with no pretense. Everything is open and naked before You, so You know all about us. You see under the makeup and the clothes, and know our hearts. Some of us are hurting and don't have the vocabulary to articulate the hurt we're experiencing. We've been bruised and battered by life, but your Word says in Matthew 11:28, "Come unto YOU, every person whose tired, worn out and heavy laden, and You would give us rest."

Father, we need rest. Many of my sisters go to bed but they don't have rest. They are taking nighttime sleep-aids but they don't have rest! Father, You said we could come to You. So, we come, just as we are. Give us Lord, what we need.

<u>Put your hand on your body</u>: *Father, you said we can lay hands on the sick and the sick shall recover. We lay hands on our own bodies and command it to line up with the way it's been designed to function. Tumors, lurking in our bodies that we may not be aware of, we bind every tumor in the name of Jesus! Fibroid tumors, dry up! My sister who suffers with chronic cramps, Father heal her. My sister with an issue of blood that continues to flow and will not stop, we command it to dry up! Father, heal her, in Jesus Name! My sister whose dealing with the spirit of infirmity, we declare you are healed!*

<u>Lay hands on your back</u>: *Back, line up and be healed, in Jesus Name! We speak strength to our backs. We command our backs to line up with the Word of God. The Word of God says, we are healed! We declare we walk in divine health all the days of our lives. Sickness and disease will not lord over our bodies.*

<u>Put your hands on your breast</u>: *I bind cancer, in the Name of Jesus! Oh God, heal us! Heal us of sicknesses and diseases that have not been detected by physicians and medical tests. Father, everything is open and naked before*

IT'S YOUR TURN NOW!

You. You are the Great Physician. You know all and see all. Father, heal our bodies of cancers known and unknown!

<u>Put your hand on your heart:</u> *Father, I pray for my sister whose suffering from a broken heart. A heart that was broken by a father who molested her; an uncle, who abused her; or an authority figure who mistreated her. I bind all of the negative effects of those encounters. Father, heal the emotional wounds that's showing up as a physical heart disease. Father, we bind heart murmurs.* <u>Speak to your own heart. Tell your heart,</u> *you will beat properly.* <u>Declare with me:</u> *my blood is flowing through my heart at the proper rate, in Jesus Name! We bind high blood pressure and low blood pressure. Bring the high blood pressure down and the low blood pressure up! God, we release the pressure, right now! Father, your Word says, to cast our care on you for you care for US! Don't let us continue to carry the pressure around with us. Help us to release it, and release it NOW! In Jesus Name!*

<u>Now take your hand and lay it on your head</u>. *Do you realize, the mind affects the rest of your body? The sickness you're experiencing in your body could very well have started in your mind? If your mind is sick, it's just a matter of time, before your body lines up with the way you are thinking:*

Father, heal our minds. Transform our minds by the renewing of Your Word. Transform our thinking and change the way we think about ourselves and life in general. We bind stinking thinking. We bring every thought into the obedience of the Word of God. Father, in those areas where doubt and unbelief have crept in, help our unbelief. Heal us Father, from the inside out!

<u>Say out loud.</u> *I will not stroke out! I will not stress out! But I will live and not die and declare the works of God! In Jesus Name! AMEN!*

Now, the Bible says, you have what you say you have. If you believe that prayer and the words you've just declared over your life, praise God for it. PRAISE GOD!

Notes

Chapter 4: THE BATH OF BITTERNESS
1. http://articles.mercola.com/herbal-oils/myrrh-oil.aspx

Chapter 5: SWEET SPICES AND PERFUMES
2. http://www.webmd.com/balance/stress-management/tc/aromatherapy-essential-oils-therapy-topic-overview#1

Chapter 9: My PERIOD
3. www.astrovera.com/bible-religion/190-bible-number-9.html

4. Biblesoft's New Exhaustive Strong's Numbers and Concordance with Expanded Greek-Hebrew Dictionary. Copyright © 1994, 2003, 2006 Biblesoft, Inc. and International Bible Translators, Inc.

Chapter 10: My PEOPLE
5. www.LiveLifeHappy.com

Chapter 12: My PROFESSION
6. www.astrovera.com/bible-religion/189-bible-number-8.html

Chapter 14: My PRICE

7. Biblesoft's New Exhaustive Strong's Numbers and Concordance with Expanded Greek-Hebrew Dictionary. Copyright © 1994, 2003, 2006 Biblesoft, Inc. and International Bible Translators, Inc.

Chapter 15: The PROMOTION
    8. www.grc.nasa.gov/WWW/K-12/airplane/lift1.html

Acknowledgements

Mother Dear

To my Mother Dear, *Missionary Wardine Mabry Gordon*, my biggest cheerleader! Thank you, Mom, for always being my greatest example of a lady. Thank you for believing in me and constantly reminding me of the call of God on my life. Thank you for telling me the story of how God healed my body of asthma as a ten-month-old baby and how, at the same time God endowed me with a special anointing that you knew would be used for His glory. Thank you for recognizing the call and being the voice of God to me when I was too young to remember that life-altering experience. Mother Dear, you are a great woman, sister, wife, entrepreneur, leader, and most of all to me, Mother! It's still Your Turn, NOW!

Covenant Sister

To my AIM covenant sister, *Pastor Marla Rowe* of Destiny World Outreach Center. I thank you for your obedience to God when you invited me to speak at your 2011 Super Model Women's Conference. Your theme for that year was "It's Your Time to Shine!" As a result of my preparation for that assignment, I became more intimately acquainted with the story of Esther. It was there, at that women's conference, that God allowed me to share so much of the revelation I've received from Esther's life and as a result, my life has never been the same. Thank you, my sister, for entrusting your influence to me and allowing my ministry gift the full freedom to flow under the leading of the Holy Spirit.

Sister in Christ

To my sister in Christ, *Toni Jackson* and the Florida Parishes Missionary Baptist Association Women's Department, I thank you. After many years of incubating the dream of writing this book, God used you and your invitation for me to speak at the women's luncheon to serve as a midwife. That ministry moment was the assistance I needed to give birth to what I believe will bless the lives of so many of our sisters as they prepare to take their turn. Thank you for trusting the recommendation of my cousin, *Tonya Mabry* to invite me, although you had never heard me speak. My sister, *It's Your Turn Now!*

Finally, I'd like to acknowledge every *Sister of Destiny* that eventually became a *Sister ABLAZE*, who allowed me over the past thirty plus years to speak into your life. It is because of you, my sisters that I have the courage to step out, step up and take my turn. It is because of you, that I have been given the awesome privilege of serving as a mouthpiece of God to encourage my fellow sisters. Thank you for trusting me and

> It is because of you, my sisters that I have the courage to I step out, step up and take my turn.

believing in me every time you attended a women's conference, Bible study, or fellowship I've hosted; listened to a cassette tape and yes, I said cassette tape, CD, or MP3 download; or watched a DVD or television program I've been a part of. THANK YOU for allowing me to speak into your lives. I can't express how much your support has meant as I have *Ignited and Fanned Flames of Hope and Possibility* in the lives of each of you. It is my humble prayer that God will continue to use me to inspire you to no longer delay your hopes and dreams, but to boldly take your turn, and take it Now!

About the Author

Alma Gordon Bamberg, is a multifaceted transformational leader, speaker, author, and entrepreneur. She has traveled for more than twenty-seven years doing the work of an evangelist. She serves as the co-founder of *Spirit and Truth World Outreach Church* alongside her husband and *Dominion Team* partner, Edwin Bamberg. Evangelist BAM has served as a featured conference speaker and has ministered at events such as the international *Women Who Win* Conference hosted by Pastor Bridget Hilliard; and co-hosted with her husband a prison satellite site of the internationally acclaimed *Woman Thou Art Loosed* Conference hosted by Bishop TD Jakes. She has also been an established co-host on the *MaxLife* Television Show for Apostle I. V. and Pastor Bridget Hilliard. Evangelist BAM is an avid seeker of the things of God. She believes she's a "climate creator" born to facilitate, activate, and assist people in an unrelenting, insistent manner discover their purpose and maximize it. Her mission is to *encourage, empower, equip, evangelize and enjoy life to the fullest*. She is the founder of *Sisters ABLAZE* women's ministries. Evangelist BAM possesses a special anointing to challenge those she comes in contact with, not to settle for mediocrity. This God-chaser, through *Alma BAMberg MINinistries*, affectionately known as **BAMMIN**, is a transformational voice *"Igniting and Fanning Flames of Hope and Possibility"*. (2 Tim. 1:6 AMP)

There is also a creative side to BAM. She has an eye and a flair for fashion and interior designing. She loves creating floral and holiday decorations, making draperies, and designing many of her clothing when time permits. She enjoys savoring beautiful flowered landscapes and loves to travel both nationally and internationally. She is truly a gifted and talented woman who seeks to live life to the fullest.

You can visit BAM's website at www.BAMMIN.org.

Also by Alma Gordon Bamberg:

"Empowering you with a Success Mentality"

Whenever you experience failure and especially public failure, the only way you will be able to try again is to be fully persuaded that *success belongs to you*. This book explores eight characteristics from the book of Joshua that are necessary for success and overcoming failure, I call them the *be-attitudes for success*.

www.ingramcontent.com/pod-product-compliance
Lightning Source LLC
Chambersburg PA
CBHW070547170426
43201CB00012B/1752